PROGI
DRES

PROGRESSIVE DRESSAGE

ANDRÉ JOUSSEAUME

J. A. ALLEN

LONDON & NEW YORK

Translated by Jeanette Vigneron

Jousseaume, André
Progressive Dressage
1. Dressage
I. Title II. Vigneron, Jeanette
636.1'08'86   SF309.5   77-30280

ISBN 0-85131-231-4

First published in France by Émile Hazan, Éditeur. This first English translation published in 1978 by
J. A. Allen & Company Limited,
1, Lower Grosvenor Place, Buckingham Palace Road,
London, SW1W 0EL,
and at
Sporting Book Center, Inc.,
Canaan, N.Y. 12029,
United States of America.

Book production by Bill Ireson.

Set in 11/13 IBM Journal by Dobbie Typesetting Service, Plymouth, Devon. Printed and bound by Redwood Burn Limited, Trowbridge and Esher.

CONTENTS

PART I

PRELIMINARY TRAINING
OF THE
YOUNG HORSE

The preliminary training of the young horse, which generally lasts one year, was indispensable in the French Army because many of the young horses had never been ridden. In addition, they had nearly always been fed insufficient quantities of oats.

The period of early training proper, must always be preceded by a period of acclimatisation. This is absolutely necessary because, with changes of climate, the horse's health will often suffer and to avoid this happening a great deal of care should be given to work and to feeding.

This period is devoted exclusively to health care. How long the period should last will depend on several factors: atmospheric conditions at the time the horse is moved, age, health, quality and breed.

If possible, the horse should be placed in an isolated stable which is well situated and well ventilated. Preferably, he should be led about outside during the most pleasant part of the day, for about one hour, at a walk and on good ground. It is important that he be led as often to the right side as to the left side of the horse accompanying him. In any case, he must be treated with a great deal of kindness and patience. Brutality must be excluded at any cost.

During this whole period, the diet must be very laxative: straw and hay (ordinary ration), oats (4 to 6 litres per day) and, if possible, a mash of barley meal and carrots at each meal. Water should always be given in an individual pail and the horse must be watched carefully for epidemic and contagious diseases and parasites, usually carried by young horses.

AIMS OF PRELIMINARY TRAINING

1. To bring the horse into good condition (health and muscle).

2. To gain his confidence and to accustom him to saddle and rider.

3. To teach him to move forward to the simultaneous

action of both legs and to turn with an opening rein.

4. To accustom him to all objects encountered in the open and make him calm and straight at all gaits.

5. To give him his first lessons over jumps.

The period of preliminary training may be shortened for those horses who have been racing or have taken cross-country tests.

However, in the case of horses sold because of accidents, such as sprained tendons, or of horses castrated after their arrival at the Remount Depot, one year of preliminary training is essential in order to avoid premature fatigue while preparing them to withstand the stress of dressage training proper.

Usually, the dressage training of a thoroughbred may begin at 4 years of age and that of a half-bred at 5 years of age. Under an experienced rider, this training may be started a little earlier.

WORK ON THE LUNGE

Preliminary training must begin with basic work on the lunge and even though this training may be incomplete, it must be sufficient to make the horse obedient while teaching him to accept the saddle and rider.

It is no longer necessary to prove the usefulness of lunge training and all saddle horses should be given this training, for it is important for a rider to be able to lunge his horse, for the following reasons:

1. In order to dominate and exercise a young horse without the weight of a rider.

2. To keep a horse fit, when, for some reason, he can neither be ridden nor driven.

3. To loosen a tense and difficult horse for a few minutes before riding him.

4. As a suppling exercise and for training over fences.

This basic lunge training will be sufficient to allow for

early lessons under the saddle and for mounting the horse when he moves freely and calmly at all three gaits on the circle, with the lunge line lightly stretched, yet with no tendency to pull or move away from the centre. In addition, the horse should move forward or stop, as soon as the instructor gives him the indication to do so. He should also be willing to move on circles of different diameters at the wish of the instructor.

Training on the lunge lays down the basic foundation of equestrian language by associating, from the beginning the voice, the click of the tongue and the whip. It is by the combined action of these various aids that the young horse rapidly comes under the complete domination of his trainer. This result can only be acquired if the trainer proceeds in a correct manner and, above all, avoids frightening the animal.

THE VOICE

The voice is used in the following manner:

1. The click of the tongue, to encourage the horse to move forward.

2. 'Whoa' to slow him down (in a quiet tone of voice, pronouncing it with a lowering of the voice at the end).

3. 'Hola' to stop the horse (in a firmer tone of voice, stressing the first 'Ho' and lowering the voice for the second syllable 'la').

THE LUNGE

The lunge is used to give indications, or to punish the horse, by use of:

1. Horizontal vibrations, to drive the horse away from the centre of the circle.

2. Vertical vibrations, to ask the horse to slow down or to stop if the voice on its own is not enough.

3. Jerks, given on the nose more or less strongly, to punish.

The whip which can be replaced by a riding crop during the first two lessons, so as not to frighten an especially nervous horse, must be handled very skilfully. The trainer must especially avoid snapping the lash and must be sure to hold the whip with the handle coming out by his thumb and the other end lying on the ground and somewhat behind him. In this way, the horse does not see the whip and cannot be frightened.

To use the whip, raise it horizontally and direct it toward the horse, bringing the thumb in and putting the elbow out. This simple motion, along with a click of the tongue, nearly always sends the horse on. When a stronger use of the lunge whip is desired (for example, in the case of punishment), it should be held with the handle coming out by the little finger and the lash of the whip should reach the horse just above the hock.

Prior to any work on the lunge line, be sure that the lunge cavesson is well adjusted, high enough not to interfere with breathing and that the noseband is well tightened so that the cavesson will not turn and injure the horse's eye with the cheek piece.

In order to start a horse off on the lunge, use an assistant who will lead the horse on a small circle while holding the cheek piece of the cavesson. The trainer holds the other end of the lunge rein (or more exactly, the length of lunge rein) folded and placed flat in his hand and not rolled around it. If the horse is turning to the right, the trainer will hold it in his right hand and if the horse is turning to the left, in his left hand. In the other hand the trainer will hold the lunge whip, as described above. The trainer is thus placed at the point of a V, the branches of which consist of the lunge line and the whip, when this is being used.

The place of the trainer is very important and, at the

beginning, he himself should move on a small circle. When the horse is moving, he should walk parallel to and in the direction of the haunches and, when he wishes to stop the horse, he should move towards the shoulder.

As soon as the horse walks quietly on the circle, the assistant ceases to hold the cheek piece of the cavesson and continues to walk along near him, patting him if necessary and then, little by little, he moves away from the horse following the lunge rein but does not turn his back to the horse. Next, the assistant can be dispensed with. Indeed, he is often not needed at all with an experienced trainer.

In order to master the horse in the beginning, it is important to work him at a walk on a small circle of some 3.5 to 4 metres diameter (beware of kicks from difficult horses). If the horse wants to let fly with his heels in the direction of the trainer, oppose the forehand to the haunches by pulling on the lunge.

When the animal performs the lunge work correctly at a walk, make him trot by stimulating him more energetically. The diameter of the circle should be increased, but work at a canter must not be undertaken unless the horse is perfectly calm and obedient at the walk and trot.

In order to begin the work at a canter, put the horse on a fairly large circle (about 10 metres diameter), so that he may canter without difficulty. When the horse canters easily on this circle, progressively reduce the diameter without slowing the rate, so that this exercise may really be a suppling effort for the horse.

At the halt, the horse must remain straight on the circle and the trainer must reward him by patting him on the haunch, taking care, however, to first walk towards the shoulder. It is preferable to pat the hindquarters rather than the shoulder, so that the horse is not tempted to follow the trainer when he returns to his place.

Thus, the elementary work on the lunge consists in

making the horse calm and obedient at the three gaits, making him move freely forward upon a voice command, changing without difficulty from one gait to another. This elementary training is necessary, yet sufficient, for most saddle horses. However, it is a good idea to further this education and one may then teach the horse to come to the trainer upon the voice command, 'Come', accompanied by a light pull on the lunge line. Then, take advantage of this exercise to ask, 'Change hands', between the circle and the instructor, who should then change over his whip and lunge. After having asked for 'Come' with the lunge, 'Change hands' is asked with the whip by raising it fairly high and to the side opposite the turn and, if this is not sufficient, by lightly tapping the neck or shoulder.

For complete training on the lunge and, in particular, jumping on the lunge, reference should be made to the book by Gontaut-Biron *Travail à la longe et dressage à l'obstacle*.

With certain difficult, or very heavy, horses the cavesson may prove to be insufficient, or may require too much effort on the part of the trainer. In such cases there is a manner of arranging the rein which I recommend and with which nearly all horses manifesting some difficulties can be rapidly dominated. The cavesson is replaced by a snaffle bridle without reins, the lunge line is passed through the inside ring of the snaffle bit, then over the neck and the end of the lunge line is snapped onto the outside ring of the snaffle bit. The fixed point of the lunge on the crest of the neck is placed farther away from the poll in proportion to the horse's degree of difficulty.

It should be noted that long reins (Mauléon reins) also give very good results. Later, they will be used advantageously as a means of suppling.

THE BIT

The bit should be mild. Therefore, use a snaffle, but do

not forget that if the bit should be mild, so should the hand. The young horse should not fear the hand of the rider and, on the contrary, it is indispensable that he has confidence in it from the beginning. The more sensitive the horse's mouth, the milder then hand should be: 'A gallant mouth to a gallant hand'.

GAINING TRUST
LESSON OF THE SADDLE

The period of gaining confidence is particularly important with difficult and timid horses, since it is a question of showing the horse that man is at the same time his master and his friend.

New horses must first learn to stand the contact of the saddle and then the weight of the rider.

Girth. The horse is easily accustomed to contact with the girth, by putting a roller on him in the stable, first loose and then gradually tightened.

Saddle. Do not begin the lesson of the saddle until the horse is docile and disciplined in the work of the lunge. In this work, avoid all brutality and clumsiness, for it is a question of the gaining of the pupil's confidence.

Have the horse brought into the riding school wearing a cavesson and use a skilful and experienced assistant. First, give the horse a good suppling exercise. Then, with the trainer holding the lunge, the assistant places the saddle lightly on the pupil's back, avoiding any rough movement and after he has stroked and patted him. Avoid dropping or throwing the saddle, the effect of which will increase the horse's fear. During this work, if necessary, bring the horse to attention by a few jerks on the lunge. Then the question of the girth is easily solved if the horse has been accustomed to the roller in the stable. First of all the girth should be only lightly tightened — this is very important — it should only hold the saddle enough to prevent it from turning. Make the horse move forward at a walk, with the assistant remaining at his head and stroking him. After walking and halting several times, the assistant moves away and the horse is asked to move off at a trot. This is often the time when some horses manifest a few defences (kicking out, bucking). Let the horse relax for a few circles. He will quickly calm down by himself; if not, punish him with a few jerks of the lunge line. It is important to force the horse to keep moving forward, so that he will not get the habit of performing his defences at a standstill.

In fact, when the horse is ridden the reactions transmitted to the rider are always much harder when defences are performed at a standstill. Thus, it is easier to dominate a horse when his defences are made when moving forward.

As soon as the horse has calmed down, stop him and stroke him, tighten the girth very gradually and begin again. Depending upon the horse, this lesson will be given several times.

Mounting lesson. Do not begin until the horse is absolutely calm during saddling. The mounting lesson is extremely important, because getting into the saddle on a horse which is difficult to mount is always a critical time for the rider.

This lesson should also be given in the riding school, the trainer holding the longe rein and the assistant performing the following movements:

(a) Put his weight on the saddle with his hand.

(b) Put his weight on the stirrup on the near side.

(c) Put his foot in the stirrup.

(d) Put the weight of the rider on the stirrup; he leans his upper body over the neck and strokes the horse with his right hand.

(e) Get into the saddle quietly.

Each of these exercises must be carried out several times while requiring the greatest calm from the horse. In general, the entire lesson can be given in one period.

With especially sensitive horses, it is a good idea not to mount by the stirrup during the first lessons and begin to accustom the horse to the weight of the rider by the rider being given a leg up, on condition that the rider knows how to do this correctly. Once in the saddle take up the reins, but do not tighten them in order to avoid any involuntary jerks. The trainer holding the lunge then puts the horse into a walk without surprising him and the rider maintains his seat while stroking the horse. Do not forget to use the voice, as in all the preceding exercises.

After a few circles on the lunge rein, stop the horse with a voice command and begin again the same procedure. Then, as soon as the horse appears to be confident, do away with the longe rein and have him follow a confirmed horse which will be used as a schoolmaster.

After this, the mounting lesson will be given without the use of the lunge. At first, an assistant may be placed in front of the horse and he may stroke the horse and give him some oats or a carrot, but under no pretext must he take hold of the reins; he may only hold the cheek piece of the bridle, above the bit.

Progressively the trainer must reach the point where he can mount the horse alone, with the horse remaining completely still. Be careful not pull on the reins when getting into the saddle.

Lesson of the legs. Also being this work on the lunge. During the training on the lunge, the horse has already associated the action of the lunge whip with clicking of the tongue; now, he must associate clicking of the tongue with the simultaneous action of both legs through the use, if necessary, of the lunge whip and the riding whip. It is a question of making the horse understand that, when the rider closes his legs, he must move forward.

The leg action takes place through the calves placed slightly behind the girth, followed immediately by clicking of the tongue and accompanied, if necessary, by the lunge whip. The action of the riding whip takes place behind the rider's legs, near the flank.

If the action of the calves is not enough, use the heels and, later, the spurs. Use little squeezes of the calves rather than strong pressure.

The lesson of the spurs must be given during early training, as soon as the horse has enough confidence in his rider. The spurs must reinforce the action of the legs in case of laziness or stubborn resistance; the horse must then respond by forward movement as he normally would to a simple squeeze of the calves. This lesson is given on the lunge, as is the lesson of the legs. Whenever a horse shows signs of resistance during the course of training, it is a good idea to repeat the lesson of the legs.

It is very important that the hand does not oppose the forward movement, so that the horse may rapidly understand what is asked of him. The contact should be light and during the first lessons it is preferable to have loose reins.

DAILY WORK

In the early stages, as soon as the leg lesson has been given, the young horses should work together in single file behind a quiet and confirmed horse.

At least two-thirds of the work should be done outdoors, in order to accustom the horses to everything they might eventually meet. In addition, this work in the fresh air will build up their health and muscles.

The outside work is done at a walk and a trot. Once or twice a week, canter the horses, for 1,000 to 1,200 metres, going no faster than 500 metres per minute. Avoid getting young horses into a sweat.

Since the weight of the rider is unequally distributed between the forehand and the hindquarters, the young horse must find his balance. Work in varied terrain, by requiring continual changes in equilibrium, is the best way to force the horse to balance himself and eventually make him handy. Do not forget that the horse, and the young horse in particular, needs great freedom of the neck each time he has to modify his equilibrium or makes a great effort (for example, climbing uphill or jumping and so on).

Therefore, the rider should, at the same time, maintain a soft contact and allow complete freedom of the neck, so that the horse may use it according to his instinct, for this will guide him better than anything the rider can do.

Also, each time the horse is given a rest, the rider should ask for *extensions of the neck*.

This suppling exercise consists of allowing the neck to relax progressively as it is lowered slightly, the hand being lowered and the fingers opening until complete lightness is obtained. In this way, the neck reaches its maximum extension, while at the same time the angle it makes with head is opened.

The extension of the neck should never be carried out abruptly, with the horse trying to pull the reins of the rider's hand. In this case, the rider must resist firmly with his fingers and then ask for another neck extension, taking care to vibrate with both hands until the end of the exercise.

As soon as progress allows, do away with the school-master lead horses, forming groups of three to four horses and taking care not to put nervous or difficult horses together.

Take advantage of the lessons in the riding school to teach the opening rein and to perfect the action of the rider's legs and, for the beginning, training on the lunge, so that work over fences may soon begin.

At the end of good early training, the horse should:

1. Be 'in front of the legs' (that is, respond without hesitation to the simultaneous action of both legs).

2. Have a soft contact with the hand without pulling. During this period do not ask for flexions, nor elevations of the neck, but make the horse 'taut' and accustom him to come honestly to the hand, which must remain low. In this way, the neck will become muscled and the trainer will avoid making it 'rubbery', which is very harmful to future dressage training.

3. Perfectly obey the opening rein.

4. Be completely trained on the lunge.

5. Be able to jump small fences on the lunge and this with the utmost calm (rail on the ground at a walk and trot, small jumps at a walk with a few trotting strides, fences of 0.5 to 0.8 metres high and small spread fences).

6. Go over small natural obstacles while ridden outdoors (tree trunks, ditches, small banks and so on).

Above all, keep the horse straight and calm, hence the necessity of jumping at the trot.

CONDITION OF THE HORSE

The condition of the horse must be the object of constant care during the early training. The following should be given particular attention:

APPETITE

If the horse lacks appetite, try everything to make him eat and seek advice from the veterinary surgeon. Have the horse's teeth examined (irregular teeth may prevent proper chewing of food) and feed two mashes per week.

DROPPINGS

Be sure that the oats the horse has eaten are well digested and the droppings contain no worms. If necessary, feed crushed oats at every other meal and, if the horse has worms, request medicine from the veterinary surgeon.

LEGS

Make sure that the legs are not affected in any way by the work done during this period. If some young horses are a bit clumsy, protect their legs with boots, in order to avoid blemishes, splints and so on.

PART II

DRESSAGE

Dressage (or training of the horse) entails a certain number of fixed principles which must be kept in mind. However, within the framework of these principles and with the use of a logical progression applicable to all horses, it still remains true that the dressage work must be reasoned out and that, at each instant, the rider must be alert and look for the causes of any difficulties encountered.

This is just what makes any new dressage project interesting and exciting, as each horse has his own personal character and reflexes, as well as extremely variable physical aptitudes.

GOAL OF DRESSAGE

The goal of dressage is to make the horse agreeable and easy to ride.

What is the definition of a horse that is agreeable and easy to ride? First, it is a well-balanced horse. If the natural equilibrium is faulty, it will be improved during the course of dressage training.

Second, if the horse submits to his rider, that is obeys the lightest indication of the rider's hands and legs, he is light to what are conventionally called the 'aids'.

A good saddle horse will, therefore, be a horse whose equilibrium gives the rider a feeling of security, who turns easily upon an indication of the reins, going forward upon the least indication of both legs and stopping upon a simple action of both hands without the need of force.

It should be noted that the perfect horse does not exist and that a good horse, even though well trained, does not move automatically like a machine; the rider must know how to command him, call him to order, and dominate him, if necessary. The mastery of a horse becomes easier with the progression of his training.

CONVENTIONAL LANGUAGE

All training is accomplished through a language

established between the rider and the horse. The first elements must be simple, precise, easy to teach and easily understood by the horse.

This language, called the 'language of the aids', will give the horse the reflexes desired by the rider. These reflexes will result in specific position and movements which will become instantaneous when the language is understood. Thus, the thought and desire of the rider will be transmitted to the horse, whose submission will increase as the rider's actions become more precise.

FUNDAMENTAL PRINCIPLES

1. The same causes always produce the same effects. Therefore, the necessity of precision in demands and always the use of the same aids for given movements.

2. Go from the simple to the complex.

3. In order to progress, look for perfection in the simple and elementary movements.

This principle is very important, for perfection of any given movement consists in obtaining execution of this movement with no contraction whatsoever. However, if there is contraction, there is resistance and if the latter is not destroyed in the simple movements it will return amplified in the difficult movements, which will inevitably lead to a refractory horse. Then it will be necessary to go back and begin again and thus waste time, for the horse will have acquired bad habits which must be erased. It is, therefore, by gradual requirements in the simple movements, according to the progress of the horse, that one is certain to go fast, though one seems to go slowly. In the beginning, the dressage training may give the impression of marking time but, later on, one will harvest the fruits of this slowness when the more difficult movements are undertaken.

4. Never ask a horse for a movement for which it is not prepared. This would bring the rider up against a lack of

understanding or an exaggerated physical difficulty.

5. Avoid the defences of the horse and delay them as long as possible. Nevertheless, the horse must not interpret this as a weakness on the part of the rider.

6. *Dominate* the horse. Do not confuse domination and brutality. One can dominate a horse without an act of brutality, whereas one can act brutally without dominating him.

7. Take into account mental faculties. The demands of the rider must be proportioned to the horse's faculty of understanding. Each demand of the rider forces the young horse to pay attention to a certain extent and this attention is proportionately greater when the reflexes are not yet educated. This results in a more rapid psychological fatigue than physical fatigue, which the rider generally does not realize.

This fatigue leads to nervousness and thence to defences, which are mistakenly construed as 'stubbornness'.

Therefore, it is necessary to give frequent rest periods and to know how to reward the horse as soon as it has done well ('done well' must be understood in a relative manner according to the stage of training).

In any case, reward is the best way of acting upon the memory of the horse, the basis of all dressage (training).

8. Do not confuse *stubbornness* on the part of the horse with *imperfections* in the demands of the rider. Such confusion is much more frequent than is generally thought. Thus the trainer, whoever he is, must begin by ascertaining that there is no fault on his part; it is indispensable that his aids act to the proper degree and at the right time.

9. During the whole course of the dressage, always remember the maxim of General l'Hotte: *'calm, forward and straight'*.

QUALITIES OF A WELL-TRAINED HORSE

1. He is calm with a maximum of impulsion.

2. His natural gaits are improved and not deformed.

3. He has a perfect equilibrium characterized by a maximum of lightness.

4. He is attentive and yet he works gaily.

5. He has a correct head position corresponding to the movement performed.

6. He performs movements perfectly without the use of force by the rider.

BITTING

The bit deserves the rider's full attention; it should be as mild as possible. For this reason, severe bits should be rejected.

During the preliminary training and the beginning of dressage training, a rather thick snaffle is the only type of bit to be used.

At the beginning of his career, Baucher used a full bridle (bridoon and curb bits). But, later on, he recommended the use of the plain snaffle even for the difficult dressage figures. Saint Phalle also recommended the snaffle up to a rather advanced degree of training.

The following principle should be observed: 'The easiest bit suitable to the horse being trained'.

On the one hand, the sensitivity of the mouth, even though Baucher holds to the contrary, is not the same in all horses; the natural equilibrium of the horse and his weight are factors which influence the choice of a bit.

On the other hand, the skill of the rider also plays an important role in this choice and it should be remarked that, if a very skilful trainer can fully train a horse with a plain snaffle this does not hold true for another less experienced rider.

These considerations show that it is indispensable to begin training with a snaffle. Nevertheless, if a horse's mouth is too contracted, one can try a double snaffle, which has a relaxing action.

During the course of dressage, as soon as difficulties are encountered with the plain snaffle, it is worthwhile to add a plain curb bit with short branches, with or without port. It is up to the rider to try each of these bits to find the suitable one. The curb chain should be adjusted so that the branches cannot be placed on the same line as the reins. When the curb chain begins to take effect, the branches of the curb bit should form approximately a 45° angle with the lower jaw. In other words, if the curb bit tilts completely the chain no longer has any effect and becomes useless; thus, the curb chain must neither be too long nor too short, for the latter would paralyse the horse's mouth and consequently there would be practically no possibility of relaxation.

Another type of curb bit is the 'sliding cheek bit' which allows a slight movement in the mouth and induces the horse to chew his bit. For this reason, it can be used advantageously with horses who have 'silent' mouths.

The snaffle (bridoon) used in conjunction with the curb bit should not be as thick as the plain snaffle. The use of the Baucher snaffle (which is suspended in the mouth) is recommended, for it cannot slide laterally in the horse's mouth and this does away with the disadvantage of the plain snaffle; that is, its lateral rein effects, the rings can enter the mouth and hurt the horse.

Some horses are heavy on the hand or have a tendency to pull in a plain snaffle. The pullers are often found among horses that have been in training and have raced. In this case, it is advisable to put them in a full bridle rapidly; this generally makes it possible to obtain a certain lightness immediately. In fact, it is useless to do without this bit, even at the beginning of dressage, if it will make training easier. However, as the training advances, the snaffle should be used more and more, while the curb reins are slightly floating. In this way, the horse's mouth becomes 'friendlier' and a softer contact is established.

AUXILIARY REINS

All auxiliary reins (martingales and others) are prohibited in dressage. In effect, the goal of dressage is to make the horse agreeable to ride without the help of all these artificial aids. Therefore, they should be used only to reinforce the strength of the rider's actions in public competition, such as races and stadium jumping, in order to make the best use of a partly-trained horse or one that presents serious difficulties. With a well-trained horse, all these auxiliaries should disappear.

CONTACT

Through the intermediary of the reins, contact of the mouth with the bit is transmitted to the hands of the rider. No matter how light one wishes the contact to be during work in the indoor school it should always exist, since it is the only means of communicating the intentions of the rider through the intermediary of his hand. Total absence of contact should never last more than a few seconds.

Contacts can be divided into three categories:

1. *Light* contact, which one must seek during work in the indoor school and which is the result of 'lightness'. This is an extremely fine contact that can exist only in a very supple horse in perfect equilibrium.

2. *Soft* contact, is slightly more marked and becomes necessary during outside work at faster paces or over obstacles. However, exaggeration should be avoided, since a good natural equilibrium is necessary in cross-country riding as well as jumping.

3. *Firm* contact, which is suitable to rapid paces (for example, racing). The horse quickly takes this contact during training gallops.

Thus, the contact differs according to the type of work

and the expression 'on the bit' can be used just as well for a light contact as for a firm contact. Do not confuse 'a horse on the bit' with a horse that 'pulls'. On the other hand, do not confuse 'a horse that goes lightly' with a horse that is 'behind the bit', that is, a horse that refuses contact and is often behind the rider's legs.

AIDS OF THE RIDER

The following are known as the 'Aids': the hands, the legs (with or without spurs), the seat and the whip.

The actions of the hands and the legs will be indicated in the course of the training programme.

SPURS

These may be used with or without rowels. Especially with mares, it is often preferable to use blunt spurs; 'tail swishing' will thus be avoided. The length of the spurs depends upon the length of the rider's leg; it should be possible to use them with a minimum displacement of the legs. On the other hand, they should not be used carelessly. Therefore, the spurs should be long for tall riders and short for smaller ones.

Spurs should reinforce the action of the legs and become a punishment for a lazy or refractory horse. Thus, from the beginning, the horse must be trained to the action of the spurs and he must be given the reflex of responding by forward movement. He must fear the spurs and yet not be terrified of them. Given the right application, the action of the spurs makes it possible to obtain more brilliancy in school figures; with a well-trained horse, a simple touch on the skin is normally sufficient.

THE SEAT

The seat of the rider is also an aid that must not be neglected, since it acts upon the horse's equilibrium. In the beginning, a good seat is indispensable in order not to upset the desired balance. Once the result is obtained, the seat takes on a very special meaning, because to a certain extent, it can modify the balance and thus become a means of action to obtain perfect execution.

How does one use the seat?

As with the other aids, the changes of seat must be practically invisible. Thus, in order to shift the weight on one side, it is necessary only to put the weight of the upper body on the seat-bone (buttock), putting more pressure of the foot on the stirrup. Do not move the upper body, because it is necessary to be able to move rapidly from one state of balance to another.

Balance depends upon the position of the centre of gravity of 'rider-horse' unit. However, the position of the centre of gravity is an imperceptible thing, while the balance resulting from this position is clearly felt by the rider. For this reason, during the course of this programme, the centre of gravity will never be discussed, only the balance to be attained.

This balance may be described as: balance on the haunches, balance on the shoulders, horizontal balance, balance on the right and on the left. It is enough for the rider to feel the state of balance of the horse and know how to modify it if necessary; the position of the centre of gravity matters little to him.

THE WHIP

This is an aid which must be used at the right moment. It can be used to reinforce either the action of the isolated leg, as will be explained later, or the action of both legs to determine forward movement. In the second case, and each time there is occasion to correct the signs of a stubborn resistance, the blow of the whip must be energetic and is given behind the rider's leg near the flank. One energetic blow of the whip is better than several mild taps.

In addition, so that the horse may understand the relationship between the punishment inflicted and the fault committed, the punishment must immediately follow the resistance.

The whip is especially necessary as an intermediate aid at the beginning of traaining; but, in more advanced stages of training, it is better for the rider not to carry a whip in order to have a greater freedom of his hands, unless he expects stubborn resistance.

GAITS

With regard to the gaits, one must consider the legs in support, the legs in the air and the time of suspension.

A leg is in support when it is upon the ground, in the air when it is raised.

If no leg is in support, this is called a period of suspension.

NATURAL GAITS

These are the gaits performed instinctively by the horse: the walk, the trot, and the canter.

THE WALK

The walk is a four beat gait. Starting with the right fore foot, the legs are lifted and grounded successively in the following order:

1. Right fore
2. Left hind
3. Left fore
4. Right hind

A walk on the right lead ends with the grounding of the right fore and a walk on the left lead by that of the left fore.

In a full cycle of the walk, there are four different periods of support which may be resumed as follows:

Walk on the right lead:

(a) Left lateral support.

(b) Support of both hind legs (right one forward), support of one foreleg (left).

(c) Diagonal support (left).

(d) Support of single hindleg (right) and both forelegs (right foreleg forward).

Walk on the left lead:

(a) Right lateral support.

(b) Support of both hindlegs (left one forward), support or one foreleg (right).

(c) Diagonal support (right).

(d) Support of single hindleg (left) and both forelegs (left foreleg forward).

THE TROT

The trot is a 'jumped' gait with a two-time rhythm, moving in diagonal pairs, there being a moment of suspension between the time of support of each pair of diagonals.

The right diagonal is that of the right foreleg and the left hindleg and, inversely, the left diagonal is that of the left fore and the right hindleg.

At the trot, there is a period of suspension between the time of support of each diagonal.

THE CANTER

The canter is a 'rocking' gait with a three-time rhythm. The horse canters to the right (or on the right lead) when the right lateral pair of legs passes in front of the left lateral pair. He canters to the left (or on the left lead) when the left lateral pair of legs pass in front of the right lateral pair.

During the canter to the right, the horse grounds successively:

1. Left hindleg.
2. Left diagonal pair.
3. Right foreleg.

The period of suspension takes place between the third and first periods described above.

The canter to the left goes as follows:
1. Right hindleg.
2. Right diagonal pair.
3. Left foreleg.

THE REIN BACK

The rein back is a two-time gait in which the horse performs by diagonal pairs of legs.

PART III

THE FIRST PERIOD

This period will be devoted to the teaching, at a walk, of the basic movements. As a rule, the trot and the canter will only be used as suppling exercises. In addition, certain easy movements will be started at a trot and will serve as a transition with the work of the second period.

THE FIRST PERIOD PROGRAMME
1. Review and improvement of the early training work.
(a) Simultaneous action of both legs. Education to be continued during the whole dressage training, in order to obtain perfect obedience to progressively lighter action.
(b) Opening rein.
(c) Transitions.
2. Study of the indirect rein.
3. Study of flexions and 2nd degree collection (*mise en main*) at the walk. Up to the half-pass at the walk and beginnings of the half-pass at the trot.

SIMULTANEOUS ACTION OF BOTH LEGS
The ideal, as stated by General l'Hotte, is to have the horse 'obedient to the breathing of the boot'.

This action must be made slightly behind the girth and preferably from back to front, first with the calf, going as far as the heel and then the spurs, if necessary.

It is important not to use continuous pressure, which would make the horse insensitive and cold to the leg. Spurs should be used in sharp, quick movements and not remain 'stuck' to the hair.

It would be a serious error to believe that at the beginning and even during the course of training, energetic legs are not necessary. One does not ride a horse without legs. Although it is necessary to seek an ever increasing lightness and arrive at a trembling of the calf or 'electric leg', it is also necessary, at each appearance of laziness or stubbornness, that the rider's legs be strong and energetic.

In short, impulsion is dependent upon the lightness to

leg aids. The result is that in increasing this lightness, impulsion is increased. This impulsion must be developed to the maximum at the walk. Therefore, before each period of rest, first ask for a few strides of extended walk then 'surrender everything' as soon as they have been obtained. It is indispensable to proceed in this way if one does not wish to rapidly have a lazy horse who works reluctantly.

At the walk, the leg aids are given alternately, each leg action being given when the hindleg on the same side is engaged. If necessary, regulate this according to the action of the shoulders (right leg action when the right shoulder moves back and vice versa). Retain contact during the extended walk, with the neck stretched out, being careful to accompany the movement of the shoulders.

ACTION OF THE HANDS

The action of the hands may be classified in three categories:
1. Active hand
2. Yielding hand
3. Resisting hand

The hand *acts* by closing fingers on stretched reins, accompanying this action with a slight elevation of the hands, particularly avoiding pulling from front to back.

The hand *yields* by opening the fingers and moving slightly forward and down or by a 'descent of the hands', as will be explained later.

The hand *resists* by forming a wall which the horse comes up against. To do this, the hand must be very steady with the fingers closed tightly on the reins. The fixed hand is obtained by tightening the elbows against the body.

DESCENT (SURRENDER) OF HANDS

The descent of hands consists of a rapid, vertical, lowering of both hands the instant the horse yields in his mouth. Contact is done away with momentarily. However, the horse must not abandon his bearing and he must retain the position he had been given. Should the contrary happen, bring him back to the original position.

DESCENT (SURRENDER) OF LEGS

In the same way, all leg action must cease as soon as obedience is obtained. This is called 'descent of legs'. The action ceases, but the leg remains in contact, ready to act again.

Thus, the descent of hands and legs are rewards for the horse, so the rider must use them frequently.[1]

RESISTANCES AND CONTRACTIONS

Before beginning the study of flexions, it should be noted that, whatever the resistances and the origin of these resistances, all resistances are expressed by contractions of the jaw. The final centre of resistance is the horse's mouth.

Resistances may be divided into 'resistances of weight' originating from bad balance and 'resistances of force' originating from muscular contractions of the jaw and directed voluntarily, or instinctively, against the acion of the bit by the horse.

The resistances of weight are contended with by the use of half-halts and resistances of force by vibrations.

The goal of flexions is to give the rider the means of destroying contractions of the mouth and, by this

---

[1] The 'descent of hands' must not be confused with the descent or relaxing of the neck. The first is a change in the position of the hands, whereas the second consists of a lengthening and lowering of the neck, thus a change of position of the horse. The descent or relaxing of the neck must take place only if the horse is at rest. If, while working, he tries a descent of the neck, this must be immediately opposed by tightening the fingers on a steady hand (the hand forms a wall).

very action, doing away with or decreasing resistance.

In addition, the goal of suppling exercises asked from the young horse will be to decrease resistances, resulting in a decrease of jaw contractions.

It may be said that flexions and suppling exercises are complementary from the beginning of training. Even during the very easy movements, perfect, or simply correct, execution can only be obtained by perfecting flexions on the one hand and suppling exercises on the other hand.

FLEXIONS AND GENERAL COMMENTS

Flexions may be asked in hand or mounted. Flexions in hand are not indispensable to many horses, but they can be extremely useful, particularly in gaining a more rapid understanding by the horse. In this way, they can decrease difficulties encountered, while the rider is mounted and lead more rapidly to correct flexions.

Either in hand or mounted, take into account the following principles:

1. Begin by lateral flexions. In these flexions, do not include the neck. Flexions of the neck recommended in the past could have been necessary with horses having thick, heavy necks, but not with Thoroughbreds and even less with Anglo-Arabs, many of which have a tendency toward 'rubber' necks.

2. Ask for the direct flexion on an elevated neck. Nevertheless, when mounted, be very progressive in the beginning as to the elevation of the neck. *One must take into account the conformation of the horse.* In certain cases, it is possible to obtain almost immediately direct flexions on a very high neck; in other cases they must be asked for only very progressively. It is up to the rider to appreciate the possible demands, but do not believe that the same elevation of the neck can be obtained with all horses, even at the end of training, since physical aptitudes are more variable.

FLEXIONS IN HAND

Flexions in hand will be sought only at the halt, following the same principles as mounted flexions. The reins are held at 10 to 15 centimetres from the mouth, and the trainer stands at the right for right lateral flexions and vice versa for left flexions; facing the horse for direct flexions.

In order to ask for a lateral flexions to the right, first use a light traction on the right rein in order to pull the head slightly toward the right; then, a light traction of both reins and wait until the horse yields in his mouth. If the yielding of the mouth is slow in coming, vibrate the left rein a few times; at the least yielding, stop all action and stroke the horse to make him understand that he has done well. Begin again several times and then, under the same conditions, ask for a few flexions to the left.

For the direct flexions, first raise the horse's head with an upward action of the snaffle. Then, when the horse is in this position, exercise traction forward to rear, keeping the neck raised and avoiding backing. If the horse does yield in his mouth, use alternate tractions to the right and the left. Yield as soon as the horse yields or begins to yield and stroke. Repeat the same exercise several times.

Lateral flexions are always asked for with the snaffle. Direct flexions can also be demanded with the curb bit, after they have already been obtained with the snaffle.

Flexion exercises must be performed at the beginning of the work period and it is advisable to repeat them at the end of the lesson before sending the horse back to the stable.

MOUNTED FLEXIONS

Mounted flexions must be asked for in the following order:
1. Lateral flexions at the halt.
2. Lateral flexions at the walk.
3. Direct flexions at the halt.

4. Direct flexions at the walk.

This lesson will first be given at the halt. The horse is more attentive, understands more rapidly, and the execution of the flexion is easier. When these flexions are well understood at the halt, they will be asked for at a walk.

Be satisfied with little at the beginning, every exaggerated demand can provoke defences which are not due to the unwillingness of the horse, but to difficulties raised by this request.

What is a lateral flexion? A lateral flexion consists of a slight rotation of the head around a vertical exis, without participation of the neck, which remains in the longitudinal axis of the horse. In other words, the hinge is between the head and neck. At the beginning, it may be necessary to allow the neck to participate slightly and to know how to adapt one's demands to the horse's conformation. Lower jaws that are too heavy are an obstacle to lateral flexions; parotid glands may be pinched, causing pain, and then defences. Therefore, it is necessary to be progressive and to know how to measure one's demands.

How is a lateral flexion demanded? Opening rein action to bring the head slightly to the right or left, then close the fingers on both reins to make the jaws yield. If the horse does not yield (which is normal at first, since he does not yet know what the rider wants), vibrate a few times with either of the reins, but preferably with the outside rein.

At the slightest yielding, reward by loosening the fingers and a descent of the hands, then stroke the horse to make him understand that this was your wish.

Normally, at the halt, if the demand has been properly made, the horse understands and easily performs this beginning of flexion, which is asked several times in a row.

At the commencement, it is important to ask for flexion with the hands held low, especially the opening rein hand;

this makes it easier for the horse.

As soon as flexions are understood at the halt, they are asked for at the walk. Of course, the reins must first be adjusted and the contact soft.

Vibrations. This name is given to vibrations transmitted to the snaffle by a rapid see-saw motion of the hand, slight in amplitude and horizontal, the fingernails underneath. The centre of this motion is the rider's wrist, hence the necessity of having a supple wrist.

DIRECT FLEXIONS

First carry out a few lateral flexions and, when the horse appears to be relaxed, ask for a direct flexion.

What is a direct flexion? It is a flexion at the poll, followed by yielding of the jaw, the head and neck remaining in the axis of the horse (i.e. straight). This flexion leads to 1st degree collection (*ramener*).

WHAT IS THE 1ST DEGREE COLLECTION?

1st degree collection is a flexion of the jaw with the addition of a flexion of the poll. The face of the horse must approach the vertical, remaining slightly in front of it, never behind. This would make the horse overbent and inevitably lead to a horse behind the bit.

HOW IS A DIRECT FLEXION DEMANDED?

1. Elevate the neck by raising the hands vertically. This elevation, especially at the walk as long as the horse has not exactly understood what is asked of him, must be as great as the conformation of the horse allows, yet without exaggeration.

2. With neck raised, tighten the fingers simultaneously on both reins. If the horse resists and hesitates to yield, encourage him to do so by vibrating with either of the reins. At the slightest yielding, descent of the hands and stroke. Repeat several times.

As the training progresses, the rider will become more demanding in asking for elevation of the neck until the neck is at the height required for 'school' work.[1]

Do not overdo when the horse has understood, for an excess of this method can start to make the horse overbent.

POSITION

The position of the horse is that which his head must take in a given movement. There are two sorts of positions.

1. The direct position called the 1st degree collection is obtained by direct flexions and, as a rule, it corresponds to the movements asked for in the direction of longitudinal axis of the horse.

2. The lateral position, called the 'bend' should be light and is asked for particularly in the work on two-tracks and at the canter.

OPENING REIN

The teaching of this rein was begun during the period of early training, but it is necessary to improve it. The goal is to obtain obedience to displacement of the hand of only a few centimetres. A simple rotation of the wrist, with the fingers up, should be enough with a well trained horse.

How does one execute an opening rein?

For example on the right rein:

1. Simultaneous action of both legs to give impulsion.

2. Move the right hand to the right and forward, with the fingernails up, keeping the elbow near the body.

3. Passive left hand.

The action of the opening rein pulls the head and neck

---

[1] To encourage the horse to yield at the poll, the rider can stroke the upper part of the neck, near the poll, either with his hand or lightly with the tip of the whip and, if necessary, using a few light taps.

to the side to which it is performed. Since this displacement of weight takes place with impulsion, it naturally causes a 'turn' to the same side. In order not to hinder the action of this rein, the other rein must remain passive and to do this, open the fingers and move the hand forward.

Because the goal of this rein is to turn the horse, impulsion must first be created; otherwise the rein will have no effect.

When moving the right hand to the right, do not forget to move it forward. Without this precaution, there would be pulling on the horse's mouth and a correctly executed opening rein must be done with no pulling from forward to rear.

It should be noted that the opening rein is a rein which we refer to as natural, because it has a direct and natural effect on the horse who cannot escape from its effect if it is carried out with impulsion. It is for this reason that the opening rein will be the first one used and care should always be taken to improve it in view of its many applications during training.

SCHOOL FIGURES TO BE USED

Changes of hand, circles, half-circles, serpentines, broken lines.

INDIRECT REIN

How is an indirect rein executed? For example, on the right rein:

1. Simultaneous action of both legs.
2. Move the right hand to the left and forward, the fingernails turned a bit upwards.
3. Passive left hand.

The effect of the indirect rein action, is to place the head to the side on which it is performed and to increase the wieght on the opposite shoulder. Thus, with the right indirect rein, the head is placed to the right and the weight is increased on the left shoulder, but this displacement of weight alone cannot cause the turn (turn to the left with the right indirect rein), because there is no direct effect on the horse as there is with the opening rein.

Proceed in the following manner:

In the half circle. Begin a half-circle with the opening rein and just as the diagonal begins, change the opening rein to the opposite rein. The horse, which always has a tendency to return to the track, will continue the movement without difficulty but, at the same time, a new reflex will begin to be formed; there will be a beginning of association between the rider's action and the movement performed. Progressively, the indirect rein will take the place of the opening rein, sooner each time, until little by little the movement can be begun solely with the bearing rein.

On the broken line. Leave the track by means of an opening rein and return to the track with an indirect rein (to the right, right opening rein and right bearing rein).

One the circle. Begin the circle with an opening rein and as soon as the horse is on the circle, use the indirect rein. For example, circle to the right, right opening rein and left indirect rein. If the horse presents difficulties while carrying out this movement, return to the opening rein to make him understand the rider's wish and then begin again with the indirect rein.

During this work, watch the impulsion, and push the horse energetically with both legs if at any time he shows the intention of slowing or stopping. In case of contraction on the indirect rein, execute a few vibrations on the rein.

ISOLATED (SINGLE) LEG AID AND DIRECT REIN OF OPPOSITION
GOAL TO BE SOUGHT

Obedience to the leg only, without the help of the direct rein of opposition.

What is the direct rein of opposition? It is a rein acting parallel to the body of the horse, with traction from forward to rear. Its effect is to increase the weight of the shoulder on the side of the rein action and to displace the haunches toward the opposite side; but its inevitable disadvantage is to reduce the impulsion, which must always be avoided with a young horse, especially when the natural impulsion is already insufficient.

This rein can thus reinforce the action of the isolated leg aid and it can be used with a trained horse, but it must not be used in teaching of the isolated leg aid, for the horse must be accustomed to displacing his haunches upon application of the leg aid only. In addition, this rein action gives the horse's head a position contrary to that which it must take during the work on two-tracks. It would, therefore, result in teaching a wrong position at the beginning of training and this would need to be corrected later.

Thus, if a right direct rein of opposition is used along with the right leg aid to demand a displacement of the haunches toward the left, the tip of the nose will point to the right. However, when the haunches move to the left, the rider should seek a slight bend to the left (*placer*), that is, to the side toward which the haunches are moving. For this reason, it is important not to give a reversed position during the first lessons and, besides this, this method does not facilitate the displacement of the haunches in any way.

METHODS

This leg action can be taught either at the halt or at the walk.

The horse understands more quickly at the halt, but at the walk he has the advantage of being in the forward movement. Nevertheless, if the rider is skilful, I believe that it is preferable to begin the first lessons at the halt. On the other hand, an inexperienced rider should begin with the horse in the forward movement. He will thus avoid having the horse anchored to the ground or backing, which inevitably happens when the rider commits faults with the action of his hands.

TRAINING AT THE HALT

1. First important point. Keep the neck straight and preferably with the tip of the nose to the side opposite the leg action. Think of the neck as a rudder. The more it is straight and rigid, the more the leg action will be efficient on the hindquarters and the sooner obedience to this action will be obtained.

2. Leg action a little behind its usual position and from front to rear. When commencing, this action should be clear, precise and energetic and if necessary, reinforced with the spurs so that the horse will quickly understand, which he cannot help but do if he is rewarded as soon as the rider has obtained a slight displacement of the haunches. The leg must act in an interrupted manner and, as the training progresses, the action will be progressively lighter until a simple trembling of the calf is attained.

With certain difficult horses, lying against the leg, it is a good idea to begin work in hand with the whip, one hand holding both reins near the mouth and maintaining the neck in the axis (i.e. straight), the other hand giving quick, little taps with the whip, behind the girth near the flank.

When the horse responds to the whip, the rider mounts and associates the action of the leg with that of the whip.

What does the *other* leg do? Placed near the girth, in contact, it maintains the impulsion. However, at the beginning, it must be passive in order to avoid confusion on the part of the horse.

If the horse shows stubborn resistance, send him forward immediately with the energetic action of both legs.

COMBINATION OF DISPLACEMENT OF HAUNCHES
WITH THE FORWARD MOVEMENT

It is obvious that during the first lessons at the halt, turns on the forehand are out of the question. The goal is simply to teach the horse to displace his haunches. As soon as this first result is acquired, this displacement must immediately be combined with the forward movement in the following manner:

Haunches-out on the half-turn in reverse. As already stated, inexperienced riders should begin with this exercise.

(a) Slow the horse at the end of the diagonal. This decrease in speed facilitates the displacement of the haunches.

(b) At the instant the horse slows, demand a displacement of the haunches toward the outside. Be satisfied with one step of the hindquarters toward the outside and complete the half-turn in reverse with the simultaneous action of both legs. Progressively reach the point where the entire half-turn is done with the haunches out.

Watch the position of the neck, which must remain straight and seek a slight bend to the side toward which the haunches are moving. Thus, the action of the hands will work to this end, in addition, making the shoulders move around the 'buckle' of the half-turn. For example, the half-turn in reverse to the right:

After slowing, action of the right bearing rein to engage the horse on the half-circle, making him turn to the left. In addition, this action places the tip of the nose to the right, light tension on the left rein and, at the same time, isolated left leg aid.

Haunches-out on the circle. When the preceding movement is easily performed, continue the same work on the circle.

First of all, take care to avoid an exaggerated displacement of the haunches which would result in preventing the displacement of the shoulders. In fact, special attention must be given to the displacement of the shoulders, which must precede that of the hindquarters. Thus, it is necessary to combine the action of the hands to obtain both the 'position' at the time of the isolated leg action and the displacement of the forehand, and this as soon as the hindquarters have taken the position corresponding to the movement of haunches-out. For example, circle to the right:

(a) Action of the left bearing rein, to demand the circle and, at the same time, the bend to the left.

(b) Action of the right leg only, to place the hind-quarters in the desired position.

(c) In certain cases, it is sometimes necessary to use light action of the right bearing rein to keep the forehand on the circle, so that the horse may perform a normal circle and to prevent him from turning on too small a circle. However, if the horse is in a state of impulsion with the right action of hands and legs, this action of the bearing rein should not be necessary.

Of course, during this last action, the left hand becomes passive and does not act again to place the horse's head until the forehand has started to move. In turn, the right hand becomes passive, on condition that the neck remains straight. This question of a rigid neck is highly important.

When should the *isolated* leg aid be used? Although it is not necessary to give specific timing applications in the beginning when the horse only obeys successive leg actions, it is important to act at the right moment as soon as the horse understands what is asked of him.

This moment corresponds to the engagement of the hindleg on the same side as that of the rider's leg. An inexpert rider should base himself on the movement of the shoulders. In fact, when the shoulder moves back, the hindleg on the same side is raised to be carried forward. In any case, the rider will quickly catch onto this timing, since the engagement of the hindleg produces a feeling of depression under his leg.

Haunches-in on the half-circle and the circle. Do not begin this work until the preceding work is easily performed; in other words, until the horse is quite obedient to the isolated leg aid. If the preceding movements have been properly obtained, the horse should have a good head position (*placer*) from the very beginning. Begin with a half-circle and, as soon as this movement is satisfactory, perform the same exercise on the circle. For example, circle to the left:

(a) Slight bend to the left (action of the left hand). With regard to the head position and the action of the bearing rein, take into account the observation made concerning the preceding movement (haunches-out). As soon as the head position is obtained, engage the shoulders on the circle by a light action of the right bearing rein.

(b) Isolated leg action on the right. This leg must act as a wall during the displacement of the forehand which follows. The effect of this first isolated leg action is to place the haunches on an inner circle. From this time on, the shoulders should move on the outer circle, displacement of the shoulders, followed by displacement of the haunches on the inner circle. Avoid too great an angle (30° to 35°).

(c) Action of the right bearing rein to move the shoulders. Proceed as for the circle with haunches-out. If the bearing rein does not suffice to displace the shoulders, the rein of indirect opposition in front of the withers 4th effect can be used temporarily, but it is indispensable to return rapidly to the bearing rein, which is sufficient if the horse is well trained to the action of this rein (see 2nd period, rein of opposition, 4th effect).

(d) Left leg at the girth, maintaining impulsion, watching over the displacement of the haunches and limiting this, if necessary.

(e) Seat to the left. The rider should always place his seat on the side toward which the haunches are moving.

Thus, on the side opposite the action of the isolated leg. However, since the rider often has a tendency to do the opposite, he should take care to avoid this error, which would hinder the balance favourable to the correct performance. In fact, it is evident that, in order to allow the lateral movement required in this work, the horse's centre of gravity must constantly be on the side toward which he is moving. The same position must also be taken in the work with haunches-out, but it takes on greater importance in the latter movement.[1]

This haunches-in work is improved by seeking a slight flexion to the inside, which is the left in the preceding example. The rider must have the feeling that the horse is bending himself around his inside leg.

HALF-PASS

The preceding work leads directly to the half-pass, all of which falls into the category of movements called 'work on two tracks'. When the haunches-in movement is performed correctly, the horse is ready to begin the half-pass. The aids to be used are the same.

STAGES OF TWO TRACK WORK

1. Half-circle with haunches-in, ending with a few steps of half-pass on the diagonal line.

2. On the track, 'head to the wall', taking care that the angle of the horse in relationship to the track does not exceed 30° to 35°. This is very important if the half-pass is to be truly performed in the forward movement.

---

[1] The hand which places the tip of the nose should preferably be higher than the other in the work of haunches-out. In the work of haunches-in, as well as in the half-pass, it is preferable that it be lower.

The forehand moves on the track of the riding school and the hindquarters on an inner track.

3. On the track, 'tail to the wall', same recommendation as above concerning the angle. The hindquarters move on the track of the riding school and this time the forehand moves on an inner track.

This movement is a little more difficult than the preceding one, because the horse is no longer guided by the wall of the riding school. It is up to the rider to guide the forehand and to keep the hindquarters on the track of the riding school.

Therefore, this work has two goals: to confirm the horse in the work on two-tracks and to teach the rider precision in his aids.

4. Half-pass on the diagonal. The forehand moves on the diagonal and the horse is practically parallel to the long sides of the riding school, but the haunches must not go beyond this parallel and preferably remain somewhat behind it.

Two main faults must be avoided..

(a) Poor head position (should not happen if the methods described have been applied from the beginning).

(b) Haunches pass in front of the shoulders. This stems from a lack of impulsion. Remedy this by alternating a few steps at the half-pass with a few steps on a straight line.

IMPULSION

The importance of impulsion must not be forgotten while doing all these new exercises. It is indispensable to give the horse the reflex of forward movement; in other words, immediate obedience to the simultaneous action of both legs. Thus, if a horse manifests stubborn resistance during the performance of a movement, do not insist upon it, but immediately use energetic action of both legs to force the horse to 'fly' forward.

Constant thought must be given to the forward movement during the whole training programme and particularly during this first period. Therefore, it is necessary to give the horse an instantaneous reflex which makes possible true impulsion and eliminates the spirit of rebellion.

Variations of pace and gait are a means of developing impulsion. During this period, the following variations should be performed:

1. Halt to a walk and vice versa.

2. Walk to sitting trot and vice versa. The sitting trot is a little slower than the medium rising trot.

3. Sitting trot to medium rising trot and vice versa.

4. Halt to sitting trot and vice versa.

On the one hand, these exercises will improve impulsion and, on the other hand, they will make the horse understand what the rider wishes through the action of both hands.

Actually, although it is necessary that the light application of both legs create the forward movement, it is just as necessary that the horse responds to the action of both hands, either by slowing or by going to the next lower gait, and this without the use of force by the hands.

At this stage of training, it is out of the question to demand halts by means which will be used when the horse's education is more advanced.

Proceed in the following manner:

(a) Relax the mouth, if necessary vibrations or small lateral flexions; in other words, seek the ramener.

(b) When relaxation is obtained, action of both hands by tightening the fingers on stretched reins and, if needed, raise the hands.

(c) Descent of legs and descent of hands. The descent of the legs precedes the descent of the hands, the latter taking place only after a complete halt is obtained. Nevertheless, the legs must remain in contact and be ready to act if the horse shows the intention of stepping back.

This principle must be observed, especially when the horse is not fully trained. In fact, the horse must not come up against a hand that is even the slightest bit hard when the rider asks for an increase in pace. This would be the best way to destroy the impulsion already acquired. In the same way, when both hands 'ask for a decrease in rate, leg action must not create confusion in the horse's mind. In order to speak in a clear language to a young horse, one must rigorously observe the principle *'hands without legs and legs without hands'*.

WORK AT THE TROT

This first period is especially devoted to training at the walk, but those movements which are well understood at the walk may be carried out at the trot.

Thus, the movements devoted to the opening rein and the bearing rein will be done at the trot (sitting trot in preference to rising trot). The work on two-tracks will be started and this will lead to the beginnings of the half-pass. The aids to be used are the same; only the gait changes.

WORK AT THE CANTER

No training at the canter during this period.

The horse will be cantered in the riding school during suppling work, or out of doors, with the neck kept long; but the training at this gait will not really begin until the following period.

However, if the horse is well balanced, not heavy and fairly supple, he can be worked at the canter on a large circle at one end of the riding school, increasing and decreasing the diameter. This work is an excellent suppling exercise.

Obviously, the horse must canter on the correct lead. To obtain a depart on the inside leg, make the horse trot on a large circle, the rider posting on the inside diagonal (inside foreleg and outside hindleg). Then extend the trot and take advantage of the end of the riding school to push the trot to its limit, so that the horse falls into the canter at the turn, which will help him to strike off on the correct lead. At the same time, use the rein of indirect opposition in front of the withers, 4th effect, on the outside. This is the canter depart by 'loss of equilibrium', which should also be used during early training.

WORK OUT OF DOORS

Training does not consist solely in work in the indoor riding school. Weather and terrain conditions permitting, go outside often, ride in varied terrain and, while riding, go over the exercises already done in the riding school. Work done outside over uneven ground calms and balances the horse. It should be done as often as possible, for the goal of training is to make the horse obedient to the wishes of his rider, under all circumstances, and not only in the riding school.

WORK PROGRAMMES (REPRISES)

In order to show the stages to be followed in the performance of the movements, the different exercises of this period are grouped into five work programmes. Do not go from one programme to another until the work in the preceding one is well understood. Each work programme may require a certain number of days, or even weeks, depending on the aptitudes of the horse and the qualities of the rider.

If a horse presents difficulties in a given moment in a work programme, it will be necessary to insist upon this movement and, in this case, the entire programme of work will not be carried out during that lesson.

LENGTH OF THE LESSON

In order to have the horse cheerful in his work, it is

indispensable not to go as far as to fatigue him. Therefore, it is preferable to give two lessons a day of 30 to 35 minutes each, rather than a single one-hour lesson. There will be much greater progress in this way.

WORK PROGRAMME B

1. *Suppling work at all three gaits.*[4]
2. *Lateral flexions* at the halt.
3. *Lateral flexions* at the walk.
4. *Direct flexions* at the halt.
5. *Direct flexions* at the walk.
6. *At the halt.* Training to the isolated leg aid.[5]
7. *At the walk.* Haunches-out on the half-circle in reverse.[6]
8. *Opening rein.* At the walk and the trot (*doubler*) and half circles.

WORK PROGRAMME B

1. *Suppling work* at all three gaits.
2. *Lateral flexions* at the halt, the walk, and the trot.
3. *Direct flexions* at the halt, the walk and the trot, seeking 1st degree collection.
4. Improve the *opening rein* and begin the *indirect rein:*
   (a) Opening rein on circles.
   (b) Indirect rein on half-circles.
5. *Haunches-out* at the walk on circles.
6. *Haunches-out* at the trot on half-circles in reverse.
7. *Alterations of pace and gait:*
   (a) From the halt to the walk and vice versa.
   (b) From the walk to the trot and vice versa.

4The suppling work may be given outside and the lesson itself in the riding school.
5 One side only may be enough for the first lesson.

WORK PROGRAMME C

1. *Suppling work.*
2. *Lateral and direct flexions* at the halt, the walk and trot, seeking 1st degree collection.
3. *Opening rein* on circles and broken lines. *Indirect rein on half-circles, circles and broken lines with return to the track.*
4. *Haunches-out* at the walk and the trot on half-circles in reverse and circles.
5. *Haunches-in* at the walk on half-circles and circles.
6. *Variations of pace and gait* from sitting trot to medium rising trot and vice versa.

For beginners, do away with work at the halt and begin with the following movement.

WORK PROGRAMME D

1. *Suppling work.*
2. *Flexions*, as previous programme.
3. *Opening and bearing reins* (without change).
4. *Haunches-in* at the walk on half-circles and circles.
5. *Half-pass* at the walk on the diagonal line of the half-circle. Head to the wall at the walk.
6. *Transitions*, from the halt to sitting trot and vice versa.

WORK PROGRAMME E

1. *Suppling work.*
2. *Flexions.*
3. *Opening and indirect reins* on circles and broken lines.
4. *Haunches-in* at the walk and at the trot on circles.
5. *Work on two-tracks at the walk:*
   (a) Head to the wall.
   (b) Tail to the wall.
   (c) Diagonal.
6. *Work on two-tracks at the trot:*
   (a) Half-pass on the diagonal line of the half-circle.

7. *Transitions* (no change).
8. *Canter* on the large circle, alternately decreasing and increasing the diameter of the circle.

PART IV

THE SECOND PERIOD

The work during the Second Period consists of:

1. Perfecting all the movements of the preceding period with 2nd degree collection.

2. Half-pass at the trot.

3. Shoulder-in.

4. Work at the canter on the circle (canter and counter canter).

5. Combined effect (*effet d'ensemble*).

OPENING AND INDIRECT REINS

These two rein actions must not be neglected. The goal is to seek complete obedience to progressively lighter hand action.

This result will be obtained in working on changes of direction with one rein, the other one remaining 'floating'. For example, going on the right hand:

Ride a broken line (from the track and back to the track), with the right rein only, first used as an opening rein to leave the track, then as an indirect rein to return to the track; the left rein entirely passive and, for this, slightly floating. In so doing, the rider will understand through the difficulties encountered that, nearly always, the rein which should be passive is not completely so. Thus, this work is very useful, not only to assess exactly the degree of the horse's obedience and to improve this obedience, but also to make the rider seek the perfect amount of action of his hand. Of course, this work can only be done with horses already responding correctly to these two rein actions, such as described in the First Period.

FLEXIONS, 1ST AND 2ND DEGREE COLLECTION

Flexions should now be easily obtained at the walk. Work on them now at the trot.

The direct flexions, as we have said, results in 1st degree collection. Since the horse gives this flexion correctly at the walk, the 1st degree collection should now be correct at this gait. The case will be the same at the trot when lateral and direct flexions have been improved at this gait.

However, since the horse must always work with impulsion, the 1st degree collection, will not be enough and it will be necessary to obtain it with impulsion: this is 2nd degree collection.

The 2nd degree collection should precede each movement. While the hands demand the 1st degree collection the legs give impulsion. At first sight, this new thought may appear to be a contradiction to the principle, 'hands without legs' and 'legs without hands'. Yet, this is not at all true, because the demand for 2nd degree collection *must not modify the pace*. The opposition of hands and legs must be made in the exact amount necessary and its effect should be to concentrate the horse's forces in such a way that, if the hand yields, the impulsion will escape forward, which will be expressed as an acceleration of the movement; if the legs yield, the impulsion which is contained between the hands and legs will escape backwards and this will be expressed by slowing if the horse is in motion or by a rein-back if he is at the halt.

A horse in the perfect 2nd degree collection is thus a horse 'at attention' ready to respond to all the rider's demands.

HALF-PASS

The half-pass at the walk is now correct. It is now time to work on the half-pass at the trot. Same progression and same observations as for the half-pass at the walk, but since the pace is faster, the crossing of the legs becomes more difficult. Some horses even touch their knees during the crossing of the forelegs. The rider realizes this in hearing the sharp noise produced. This fault disappears as the horse improves in suppleness, but care must be taken to demand very little at the beginning from the point of view of the angle to help the horse in crossing his legs. Pay particular attention to the impulsion and do not forget that, as with the walk, the rider's seat must be on the side toward which the horse is moving. Give a good isolated leg aid at the time of engagement of the hindleg on the same side, this phase being more difficult to feel than at the walk.

REINS OF INDIRECT OPPOSITION
4TH AND 5TH EFFECTS

The rein of indirect opposition, 4th effect (on the right, for example), is directed from right to left passing in front of the withers and is drawn in that direction.

This action results in the following:

1. The head is brought to the right and the neck is curved toward the right.

2. The weight is placed on the left shoulder.

3. The forehand is drawn to the left and made to turn (pivot) around the haunches.

The rein of indirect opposition, 5th effect, goes behind the withers instead of in front of them, approximately in the direction of the opposite haunch.

Its effect is to move not only the forehand, but the entire horse toward the left side with the use of the right rein, and vice versa with the left rein.

SHOULDER-IN

It is now time to begin the 'shoulder-in'. In my opinion, it is useless to do it earlier. The shoulder-in must not be used to teach the isolated leg action, as some recommend. I see no need at all for this, but I do see the serious disadvantage of giving an incorrect bend to the horse. In addition, I have set forth the principle that the horse must obey the action of the isolated leg without the help of the rein of opposition, which is not the case with the shoulder-in.

On the contrary, since the horse has become very

obedient to the isolated leg action, the early stages of the shoulder-in will be made much easier, for the rider can now make use of this leg action to reinforce the rein action.

The goal of the shoulder-in is to supple the horse in his entire length, suppling of the shoulders, suppling of the spinal column, suppling of the hindquarters and engagement of the hindlegs. It is also a means of domination, but it is not the universal remedy, and although this exercise is very useful in training, in itself alone it is not enough to obtain a well-trained horse.

In order that this movement be well done, it is necessary to seek a light and regular bending inward from the head to the tail. The first shoulder-in exercises will be demanded on the circle to make this work easier for the horse. The aids to be used, going on the left hand, are as follows:

1. Left opening rein to bring the head, neck, and shoulder toward the inside of the circle.

2. Transform this opening rein into a rein of indirect opposition, 5th effect.

3. Accompany the action of this rein with a left isolated leg action. The right leg maintains impulsion and watches over the haunches.

4. Seat to the right.

With a confirmed horse, the rider should have the feeling that the horse is bending himself around the rider's inside leg, for, as training progresses, the isolated leg action should disappear, and the impulsion then being given by both legs; the action of the rein of opposition will channel this impulsion to transform it into a shoulder-in.

FAULTS TO AVOID

1. Too much bending of the neck. One must limit this curving with the passive rein (right rein in the above case) by closing the fingers on this rein as soon as the desired 'degree' of bending is reached.

2. Too great an angle of the horse in relationship to the

direction being followed (about 30°).

3. Bad position of the rider. The seat must always be on the side toward which the horse is going.

Note that the desired angle may be regulated in two ways:

(a) Either by action of the rein; this is a question of getting the proper amount of action of the 5th effect rein in relationship to the resistances encountered and according to the results obtained, in order to obtain the desired angle. It should be noted that with the same horse, these actions are always more or less different on each side.

(b) Or by the outside leg, which limits the displacement of the haunches and, at the same time, forces the horse to bend around the rider's inside leg, which becomes very easy as soon as the shoulder-in is demanded with equal leg aids. It will take only a preponderance of the inside or outside leg to correct the position of the haunches, if this necessary.

PROGRESSIVE SHOULDER-IN DEMANDS

On the circle. Only a few steps at the beginning and end by pushing the horse forward on the circle.

On the track of the riding school. The forehand is on the inner track parallel to the wall, as for the movement 'tail to the wall', but the horse is bent in the opposite direction. End the movement by pushing the horse in the direction of his shoulders and make a circle which will bring him back to the track.

In any direction. Watch over the impulsion in order to avoid an exaggerated angle.

WORK AT THE CANTER

Canter on a large circle (diameter equal to the small side of the riding school), decreasing and increasing the size of the circle *without changing rate*. This work may have been started with some horses during the First Period. The canter depart is demanded by loss of equilibrium, as was described in that period. When the horse has become sufficiently supple and obedient in this exercise, the rider can demand decrease of speed on small circles, seeking 1st, and then 2nd, degree collection.

At the same time, demand a regular *placer* of the horse at the canter, which consists of a slight 'bend' to the side of the leg on which he is cantering. This bend is important, for later on it will become an indication for the horse to take a canter depart as well as to change leads.

At each stride of the canter, the hands should act by tightening the fingers on the reins between the third and first phases, and yielding between the second and third phases, so that the horse does not come up against the hand at the time he grounds the foreleg which ends the canter stride. The hand on the bend side should be slightly higher than the other.

The decreases in speed will then be demanded on the track; normal canter on the long side, slower canter on the short side. In the beginning, the rider can associate the action of the hands with the voice; to demand slowing, 'Ho' pronounced with the desired intonation will often avoid using force with the hands and will make the horse understand sooner what is asked of him (the voice has already been used in the work on the lunge, hence the new association is easy to create).

As soon as the decreases in speed are easily obtained, begin work on circles (approximately 10 metres in diameter). In this work, improve the decreases in rate and the 2nd degree collection and as soon as the horse performs these circles correctly, without being heavy on the hand and without pulling, the time has come to begin the counter canter.[1]

---

[1] In the canter, one lateral is ahead of the other and it is, therefore, necessary to ease the weight by placing the seat on the opposite side (for canter to the right, seat to the left and vice versa for the canter to the left.)

COUNTER CANTER

It is a good idea to begin the counter canter as soon as possible, because it is an excellent suppling exercise and, by giving more work to the difficult side, both sides can finally be made about equal.

The preparation for the counter canter is carried out by doing slight counter changes of hand the whole length of the long side, the horse being in 2nd degree collection and going at a sufficiently slow speed.

At first, move one or two metres away from the track, start the counter change of hand at the beginning of the long side, and ride a diagonal line, very gradually going away from the track until the centre line is reached, which marks the change of direction to be made. This change of direction must be performed quietly to avoid a change of lead or, which is more frequent, that the horse canters disunited. If necessary, flatten out the angle of the counter change of hand by cantering parallel to the long side for a few metres. In this case, the change of direction will be made in two stages, which makes it possible to avoid changing leads with horses showing some difficulties when commencing this excercise. It should be noted that this difficulty is generally encountered on one side only of the horse. The outside leg (left leg on the right hand) watches over the haunches and intervenes rapidly should there be an attempt to change leads.

The neck must remain straight with normal *placer* (right bend on the right hand). However, if the horse presents serious difficulties, the leg action can be reinforced by a direct rein of opposition on the same side, which forces yielding to the hand which demands the bend. But this should only be momentary and the goal must to be prevent a change of lead solely by preponderance of the outside leg and, later, by the 'bend' alone when the horse has learnt the habit of changing leads only when the rider changes the bend.

1. Counter change of hand, first moving away from the track very little, progressively going as far as the centre line.

2. A half-circle far enough away from the short side to give the horse time enough to balance himself before going into the turn. As training progresses, perform the half-circle nearer the short sides in order to increase the difficulty.

3. Change of hand on the diagonal, being careful in the beginning not to end up too near the turn for the same reason given in (2) above, and then go around the track a few times at a counter canter.

4. Counter canter on large circles, progressively decreasing the diameter of these circles according to the horse's progress.

5. On the figure eight. Excellent suppling exercise, the horse going alternately from the inside lead on one circle to a counter canter on the other circle.

This work should not present any serious difficulties if the progression has been followed correctly, doing each exercise on both hands. If, when going on to the next stage of training, difficulties are too great, it must be deduced that the rider wanted to go too fast. In this case, return to the preceding exercises and improve them.

COMBINED EFFECT

The combined effect is extremely useful when the rider intends to go to the highest levels of dressage training. One can even say that it is indispensable.

But, it is a two-edged knife which can have the disadvantage of making the horse cold to the legs and even refractory if it is poorly taught. Therefore, an inexperienced rider must go slowly and make sure that the impulsion is not affected.

As its name indicates, it must have a repercussion on the whole horse and put him at the entire disposal of the rider.

Therefore, its result is to dominate the horse and to calm him. Namely, it makes it possible to dominate the fear of a horse frightened by something.

HOW TO DEMAND COMBINED EFFECT

During this period, it will only be demanded at the halt.

1. Tightening of the fingers of both hands on lightly stretched reins, and then wait for the result of the action of both legs.

2. Leg action must be given at the girth, that is a little farther forward than the place used for giving impulsion. This is important, to avoid any confusion of the horse at the beginning and to avoid destroying, by this very fact, the impulsion obtained through several weeks or several months of work.

The legs act by progressive tightening, starting at the calves and going as far as the spurs, if this is necessary. At the slightest yielding of the jaw, descent of hands and descent of legs.

The result of the combined effect is expressed by 1st degree collection, all contractions ceasing in the mouth and at the poll.

If, at the beginning, the horse does not understand and remains inert, show him the rider's wish by a few vibrations, but, above all, do not increase the action of the hands which only wait for the yielding to happen. Later, the simple closing of the legs at the girth with the reins lightly stretched should cause the flexion of the poll and the jaw. In that case, the rider has the feeling that the horse is completely submitted to his wish.

Also ensure that the horse remains in the position obtained by the combined effect following a descent of the hands and legs. He should not stretch out his neck or relax it unless the rider authorises him to do so. This will be indicated by a few vibrations on long reins.

TRANSITIONS

The preceding exercises should not make the rider forget the importance of transitions as well as the pre-occupation with impulsion. The demands made during the first period must be continuously improved and sharper and more rapid transitions must be sought; in other words, a greater obedience to the action of the legs and hands.

Begin extensions at the trot (rising trot), the horse having a soft contact with the hand, the reins equally stretched, the neck quite straight to avoid striking off into a canter. The legs should exert all the necessary energy, at the same time, graduating their action in accordance with the horse's temperament and the hands should have only a soft contact. It is important to allow the horse to lengthen his neck a little. Each increase in stride, whether at the walk, the trot, or the canter, requires this slight extension.

The decreases in speed should be demanded without jerks and without forceful effects. The legs gradually cease their action, while the fingers are tightened on the reins and the wrists are raised slightly (action of the active hand.) If the horse shows resistance, the action of the hands should not be given simultaneously on both reins, but alternately on one rein and then the other.

SLOW WALK AND TROT

Work on these two gaits, seeking the maximum decrease in speed compatible with the degree of training.

At the slow trot, take care that the horse does not move at the 'amble', which often happens with horses which are lazy in their hindquarters.

EXTENDED WALK

The walk is perhaps the most difficult gait to improve. Therefore, a great deal of importance should be given to it during training.

With a cold-natured horse, it is a good idea to go on

rides with another horse which has a good walk, for, when urged energetically with both the rider's legs, he will try not to let himself be passed. On the contrary, with a hot-natured horse, it is preferable to go out alone or accompanied by a calm horse which has about the same walk, in order to avoid jogging caused by nervousness.

If the horse is calm, seek to extend the walk to its maximum when returning to the stable in order to exploit the natural tendency of attraction to the stable. However, with nervous horses, this generally takes the form of jogging, which the rider must try hard to fight and this often requires a great deal of patience and calm. A few steps of shoulder-in on each side nearly always give good results, but it is necessary to do this at each attempt at jogging.

RESULTS AT THE END OF THE PERIOD

Perfect 2nd degree collection at the walk and the trot and its beginning at a slightly slower canter.

1. Very good half-pass at the walk and trot.

2. Transitions more supple and with quicker response.

3. In the decrease in rate, horse light to the hand, going easily into 2nd degree collection.

4. The halts are still done progressively, but more rapidly and without jerking, the horse remaining in 2nd degree collection the gait 'dying out' gracefully with suppleness.

5. The shoulder-in is performed easily at the walk and is begun at the trot.

6. The canter is beginning to go slower with no difficulties and this with a beginning of 2nd degree collection. The horse should be able to canter easily on smaller circles (8 to 10 metres diameter).

7. Counter canter several times around the riding school and on the circle.

8. Combined effect well understood at the halt.

WORK PROGRAMME A

1. *Suppling work at three gaits.* Canter on the circle, varying the diameter while, at the same time, remaining at the same rate.
2. *Opening and indirect reins.* Broken line with opening rein to leave the track, and indirect rein to return to it, the other rein completely passive and slightly loose.
3. *Work on two tracks:*
   (a) At the walk:
      — Haunches-in
      — Head to the wall
      — Tail to the wall
      — Half pass on the diagonal.
   (b) At the trot:
      — Haunches-in
      — Half-pass on the oblique line of the half-circle
      — Head-to-the-wall
4. *Transitions:*
   (a) Begin the slow walk.
      — Slow trot and extended walk.
5. *Flexions*[2]

WORK PROGRAMME B

1. *Suppling work:* Slow the canter on small circles.
2. *Opening and indirect reins* (without change)
3. *Work on two tracks*[3]
   (a) At the walk (without change)
   (b) At the trot:
      — Haunches-in
      —Half-pass on the oblique line of the half-circle.
      —Head to the wall.
      —Tail to the wall.
4. *Transitions* from extension of rising trot on the long sides of the riding school.

WORK PROGRAMME C

1. *Suppling work* (without change).
2. *Opening and indirect reins* (without change).
3. *Work on two tracks:*
   (a) at the walk (without change)
   (b) At the trot:
      — half-pass on the diagonal of the riding school.
4. *Transitions* from slowing of canter on small sides of the riding school.
5. *Shoulder-in.* At the walk on the circle.

WORK PROGRAMME D

1. *Suppling work*[4] (without change).
2. *Opening and bearing reins.* Broken lines and voltes at the slow walk and slow trot.
3. *Work on two tracks* (without change).
4. *Transitions:* Begin circles at the canter, going as slowly as the horse's degree of training allows (10 metres diameter).
5. *Shoulder-in:*
   (a) At the walk on the long side.
   (b) At the trot on the circle.

WORK PROGRAMME E

1. *Work on two tracks* (without change)
2. *Combined effect.* At the halt.

---

[2] Reference will no longer be made to lateral and direct flexions, but they should be continued at the beginning of each lesson and each time there is a contraction.

[3] Return to *haunches-out* on the circle each time the horse becomes lazy in his response to the isolated leg, as well as to improve the 2nd degree collection.

[4] Reference will no longer be made to suppling work, nor to opening and indirect reins (to be continued without change).

3. *Transitions*
   (a) Special attention to slow walk and slow trot.
   (b) Extended trot more strongly marked.
4. *Shoulder-in:*
   (a) At the walk (without change)
   (b) At the trot: on the long side.
5. *Canter.* Try to decrease the diameter of the circle, on condition that the horse remains light.
6. *Counter Canter.* Counter changes of hand (very slightly pronounced at the beginning, to arrive progressively at the centre point).

WORK PROGRAMME F

1. *Combined effects.* At the halt.
2. *Work on two tracks.* Increase the extent of crossing over.
3. *Transitions.* Special attention to the extended walk.
4. *Shoulder-in* (without change).
5. *Canter.* On circles as small as the degree of training and conformation of the horse allow.
6. *Counter Canter.* Following a half-circle and several times around the riding hall.

WORK PROGRAMME G

1. *Combined effect.* At the halt.
2. *Work on two tracks* (without change).
3. *Transitions:*
   (a) Try to increase the length of the stride when extending the trot.
   (b) Special care to slowing of rates.
   (c) Extended walk.
4. *Shoulder-in* (without change)
5. *Canter.* Special attention to work on circles.
6. *Counter canter:* Starting from a change of hand through the diagonal and as soon as possible on the large circle.

MODEL WORK PROGRAMME
(End of Second Period)

This work programme may be divided into two lessons of approximately 30 minutes each, given during the same day, instead of a 60 minute lesson. In this case: 1st lesson from Nos. 1 to 8 inclusive; 2nd lesson beginning with No. 9. The slow walk and trot may be demanded during transitions. The extended walk is demanded for a few strides before each rest.

1. Suppling work at the walk, trot, and canter   6 minutes
2. At the walk, long reins (rest)   2 minutes
3. At the walk, lateral and direct flexions
   At the trot, lateral and direct flexions   3 minutes
4. At the walk and at the trot:
   Circles, half-circles, broken lines with opening
   and indirect reins   4 minutes
5. At the walk, long reins (rest)   1 minute
6. *Effet d'ensemble* at the halt   1 to 2 minutes
7. Work on two tracks:
   a) At the walk   4 minutes
      — One circle on each hand with haunches-in
      — A few steps of head to the wall (on each hand)
      — A few steps of tail to the wall (on each hand)
      — Half-pass on the diagonal (on each hand)
        Rest   1 minute
   b) At the trot   3 minutes
      Same work as at the walk.
8. At the walk, long reins (rest)   2 minutes
9. Canter (on both hands)   3 minutes
      — Canter depart on the circle (by loss of equilibrium)
      — Lengthening (or extensions) on the long sides and
        slowing on the small sides
        Rest   1 to 2 minutes
      Circles at slow canter (on both hands)   3 minutes
10. At the walk, long reins (rest)   2 minutes

11. Shoulder-in at the walk and at the trot on
    the track   2 minutes
      Rest   1 minute
12. Transitions   4 minutes
    — From the walk to sitting trot and vice versa.
    — From the sitting trot to the halt.
    — From the halt to the sitting trot.
    — Extended trot on the long sides and slow trot
       (sitting) on the small sides.
13. At the walk, long reins (rest)   2 minutes
14. Counter canter (3 minutes on each hand)   6 minutes
    — One or two counter changes of hand on each hand.
    — Change of hand on the diagonal, going once or twice
       around the riding school or on the circle at the
       counter canter.
15. Return to calm, at the walk, on long reins   4 minutes

PART V

THE THIRD PERIOD

The following work will be covered during the Third Period:

1. Work on two tracks. Counter changes of hand at the walk and the trot.
2. Shoulder-in at the walk and the trot.
3. Turns on the forehand and on the haunches.
4. Work at the canter:
    (a) Slowing the canter.
    (b) Counter canter on progressively smaller circles.
    (c) Half-pass.
    (d) Canter departs.
5. Combined effects, at the walk and at the trot.
6. Improvement of transitions: the rein-back.

WORK ON TWO TRACKS, COUNTER CHANGES OF HAND

When this period of training is reached, the half-pass should be performed very correctly, whatever the aptitudes and the character of the horse. The difficulty should now be increased by performing counter changes of hand while at the half-pass.

In view of the fact that this movement consists of two successive half-passes, the second of which is performed in the opposite direction of the first, the difficulty, and thus the delicate moment, is manifested at the moment of the change in direction. This change from one half-pass to another is obtained in the following manner:

1. Change the *placer* and engage the shoulders in the new direction by changing the indirect rein.

2. As soon as the shoulders have begun the movement, reverse the leg action. It is important that the new isolated leg action (single leg aid) should take place only after the forehand is engaged in the new direction; without this precaution, the haunches would precede the shoulders. Consequently, if the half-pass is correct in the initial direction, the forehand is slightly in advance of the hindquarters. Therefore, at the moment of the change of

direction, the forehand must first be placed in the position which it must occupy during the new half-pass.

This change of direction must be done in suppleness, smoothly and gracefully. To do it this way, the rider must be progressive in the action of his aids, including the changing of seat. It is equally indispensable that the horse must not be surprised, as for all movements, hence the necessity of warning him.

In the work on two tracks, the change of *placer* will be the signal for 'attention' and the horse will then be ready to respond immediately to the action of the indirect rein, which will carry the forehand in the new direction, and then, to the action of the isolated leg, which will have the same goal in regard to the hindquarters.

Therefore, the whole difficulty in this figure resides in the linking of the two-half-passes, which must be obtained without a moment at halt.

When these counter changes of hand are performed correctly, the work on two-tracks may be varied as follows:

While at the tail to the wall on the long side of the riding school, on the right hand, for example, move across the riding school, remaining on two-tracks and, upon arrival at the other side, take the track to the left, continuing by the movement of head to the wall for a few meters.

Then straighten the horse by putting the shoulders before the haunches and not by putting the haunches behind the shoulders.

As the training progresses, each section will be shortened and the line ridden to go from one track to the other will be in the form of steps.[1]

---

[1] Do not forget to change the seat at each change of direction.

SHOULDER-IN

Perform at the trot the work which was performed at the walk during the preceding period.

When the horse does this exercise easily, the rider should feel the supple hindleg slide under his body.

Then try to do this without isolated leg action, having both legs equal, or with preponderance of one or the other leg to correct imperfections.

TURN ON THE FOREHAND (*Pirouette Renversee*)

First begin with a half-turn on the forehand.

One of the forelegs acts as a pivot in this movement. When the haunches move toward the right, the left foreleg acts as a pivot; in the opposite case, it is the right fore. Simply remember that there must be no backward movement. For instance, in the first case, if the horse pivots around his right foreleg, the left foreleg would have to move to the rear in order to describe a circle around the pivot. Thus, there would be a backward movement, which would be a fault.

The rider's actions for a displacement of the haunches to the right are as follows:

1. Right indirect rein which gives the bend to the right, and, at the same time, weights the left foreleg, which must serve as a pivot. Left rein slightly stretched to prevent the neck from bending. This is a question of the proper degree, which the rider must feel, so as not to hinder the principal action.

2. Left isolated leg action at the moment when the left hind leg is engaged. The rider has learnt to feel this time exactly with the work on two tracks.

3. Right leg at the girth watching over the displacement of the haunches and the impulsion to prevent any stepping back.

4. Seat to the right.

The horse has been suppled enough by the work on two-tracks so that the rider may require, from the beginning, that the left hindleg (in this case) cross easily in front of the right hindleg, and he is not satisfied to have the left hindleg simply move nearer, as often happens with horses which are lazy in their hindquarters.

Normally, the front pivot can, and even should, be slightly lifted from the ground at each step, but it should return to the same place.

TURN ON THE HAUNCHES (Pirouettes)

Begin by the half turn on the haunches.[2]

The horse is prepared by half-circles with haunches-in of a progressively smaller diameter (1 metre to 50 centimetres for the inner circle.)

Note that the hind pivot (right hindleg for the turn to the right) must not remain motionless and 'stuck' to the ground. It should be lightly raised at each step and be put down in the same place. This is indispensable, not only so that the turns on the haunches will be correct, but also to obtain mobility of the hindlegs, which is important for Haute Ecole work.

When first commencing this exercise, allow the hindlegs to move round a small circle to avoid any stepping backward, or stopping with the hindlegs, a major fault. The aids to be used are the same as those for the haunches-in movement, shown here for the right turn on the haunches.

1. Bend to the right (placer).

2. Left indirect rein to displace the shoulders to the right.

3. Left leg preponderant at the beginning of the movement, and forming a wall to prevent any movement of the haunches to the left. The right leg at the girth.

---

[2] The half-turn on the forehand should be demanded on an inner track and not on the track, so that the horse's head is not bothered by the wall.

4. Alternate actions of the legs to demand and keep up the mobility of the hindlegs, at the same time maintaining a slight preponderance of the left leg.

In a correctly performed turn on the haunches, the horse must bend himself around the rider's inside leg (the right leg in this case.)

CANTER

Take special care in extending and slowing the canter.

The extensions should be well marked by a slightly faster canter than the ordinary canter, but without exaggeration at the beginning, in order to remain master of the horse and of his balance.

In the slow canter, the action of both hands must not be simultaneous. At each stride of the canter, an alternate action of the hands must take place in the following manner (in the canter to the right, for example).

1. Action of the right rein at the end of the third phase (grounding of the right foreleg), ceasing after the first phase (engagement of the left hindleg.) The horse's mouth must not meet the hand at the beginning of the third phase.

2. Action of the left rein at the time the right rein ceases its action, that is, in the second phase (grounding of the left diagonal), ceasing before the third phase.

This results in a slight descent of the hand during the third phase, and, due to this fact, we see that, at each stride of the canter, it is necessary to 'take' and to 'give'.

These actions of the hands are executed by softly tightening the fingers; jerks on the mouth are taboo. The action of the hand on the rein must be like that of a hand kneading putty.

There is also an alternate action of the legs. The action of each leg corresponding to the engagement of the hindleg on the same side. The impulsion must be proportionately greater as the canter is slower; thus, with some cold natured horses, the legs must be particularly active.

From this time on, the question of the *'straight horse'* at the canter takes on serious importance, but the fact is that all horses canter in a more or less diagonal position, always more accentuated on one side. Therefore, it is necessary to fight this natural fault by bringing the *shoulders before the haunches* by means of the rein of indirect opposition, 4th effect, taking effect slightly before the second phase. By doing this, the horse will canter absolutely straight on both sides.

COUNTER CANTER

Work at the counter canter must be done on circles of progressively smaller diameter, as well as on the figure of eight.

Pay attention to the following points:

1. Be sure to keep the bend to the correct side (*placer* to the right for the canter to the right).

2. As training progresses and when the horse does a counter canter with no contraction whatsoever, try to mould the horse around the curve, that is, seek a light curving of the spinal column *while maintaining the placer* on the correct side. The horse then gives the feeling of bending slightly around the rider's leg, which is on the inside of the circle.

As a rule, this result will not be obtained until the end of training when the horse is supple at a slow canter, with no contraction and perfectly light.

SERPENTINE AT THE CANTER

The serpentine at the canter is an excellent exercise to supple the horse, because it goes successively from the true canter to the counter canter and vice versa. In order to be done correctly, this exercise requires a very supple horse, because the rider must try to mould the horse around the curve without modifying the *placer*.

HALF-PASS AT THE CANTER

The half-pass at the canter should be started as soon as the horse can easily maintain a slightly slowed canter. Usually it does not present any serious difficulties, since it consists of a succession of leaps while advancing across the diagonal. Normally, it can be done only at the true canter (canter to the right for the half-pass to the right). The faults to be avoided are the same as those indicated for the walk and the trot. Follow the steps given below:

1. At the end of a half-circle, demand a few strides of half-pass on the diagonal.

2. Head to the wall.

3. Tail to the wall.

4. On the diagonal of the riding school.

The actions of the aids are for example, as follows for a half-pass to the right:

1. Bend to the right (*placer*, thus corresponding to the canter on the right lead.)

2. Action of the left indirect rein, or more often the rein of indirect opposition, 4th effect. The indirect rein, 3rd effect, can have sufficient action only on horses which are really light to the hand. This action, the goal of which is to push the forehand toward the right, must take place slightly before the second phase. The instant is easy to recognize, if the rider has taken the habit of doing the slow canter with alternate hand actions, which has already been indicated.

3. Preponderant left leg, acting between the third and first phases, that is, immediately after the action of the right hand, which takes place at the end of the third phase, as was indicated for the slow canter.

4. *Seat more to the right.*[3]

---

[3] As at the walk and the trot, the half-pass at the canter must be carried out in the forward movement. Thus, the inside leg (right leg in this case) will be in charge of keeping up impulsion by acting at the time of the engagement of the right hindleg, that is, between the first and second phases. If the horse lacks impulsion at any time, send him directly forward by energetic action of both legs.

CANTER DEPARTS

All these exercises, slow canter, counter canter, serpentines at the canter, have made the horse handy and supple at this gait. He is now ready for the canter depart by the 'taking of equilibrium'; whereas this was previously demanded by the 'loss of equilibrium'.

Steps to follow:

1. Canter depart from sitting trot on the circle.
2. Canter depart from sitting trot on the straight line.
3. Canter depart from the walk on the circle.
4. Canter depart from the walk on the straight line.[4]

AIDS TO BE USED

When commencing, the aids used are not the same as those which will be used at the end of training. There is a conventional language to be established between the rider and the horse.

The actions must be excessively clear and precise at the beginning, so that the horse may easily understand. Later, the goal will be to obtain a canter depart (to the right, for example), solely by a light indication of the right rein and action of the inside leg (right leg).

However, at first, the aids to be used are as follows: *Depart on the right lead.*

(a) Right rein to demand the bend to the right, and seat to the left to unweight the right lateral.

(b) Light tension on the left rein to limit the curving of the neck.

(c) Preponderant left leg acting as an isolated leg.

(d) Right leg. The action of the left leg results in displacement of the haunches toward the right. The right

---

[4]On the straight line, begin preferably with the outside lead as soon as the horse has understood the mechanics of the canter depart.

leg intervenes at the girth (without discontinuing left leg action) at the instant when this displacement is going to take place to transform it into a forward movement at the canter.

(e) At the same time, slightly close the fingers on the right rein while raising the right hand a little. This action may give the rider the impression from which comes the expression, 'to pick up the forehand'. However, the rider cannot have the pretension of picking up the forehead. Actually, this action of the hand, which must be light and discreet, is only an indication for the horse, but indication enough to create the reflex due to the fact that the horse is placed in a position and equilibrium which are favourable to the canter depart.

(f) Yielding of both hands at the instant of the depart. The horse should not come up against the hand.

At this stage of training, if correctly demanded; the canter depart should pose no difficulties and should be rapidly understood; the slow canter and other exercises at the canter having made the horse attentive. In addition, the bend which was demanded in the preceding work at the canter has already accustomed the horse's reflexes to the action of the hand on the side of the *placer*.

Ask only a few canter departs in the same lesson and, if necessary, work on one side only in the first lessons. Later, give more work to the difficult side.

As the training progresses and when the horse no longer hesitates, the outside leg (left leg in this case) will become less and less preponderant up to the point of disappearing to obtain the depart with both legs equal and a simple action of the right rein.

AT WHAT INSTANT SHOULD THE CANTER DEPART BE DEMANDED?

For example on the right lead:

From the trot. When the right diagonal is grounded. In

fact, when this diagonal is grounded, the left hindleg can immediately begin the first stride of the canter when it pushes off. The left diagonal, being off the ground, is ready to mark the second phase, and the right foreleg, following the push-off of the left hindleg, has extended its movement and is in position to mark the third and last phase of the stride.

From the walk. When the left hindleg is in support, for the same reason as in trot (second supporting phase of a walk stride to the left), that is, when the right shoulder moves back.

From the rein-back. When the right shoulder moves back. Actually, at this time, the right diagonal is going to be grounded, and then the left hindleg can give its push-off.

COMBINED EFFECT

Now that the combined effect is well understood at the halt, it is demanded at the walk and then at the slow trot.

It is important that the gait must not be modified by the combined effect. The rate should become neither faster nor slower.

TRANSITIONS

Improve the variations by seeking a more rapid change from one gait to another while, at the same time, avoiding brutal changes. Going faster or slower must always have a certain progressiveness, a certain softness, giving the observer the impression of ease, suppleness and grace.

Work particularly on the slow walk, the extended walk, the slow trot and the extended trot. Seek active hindlegs at the slow walk and trot. Nearly always, these slow gaits show a lack of activity of the hindquarters, in other words, a certain laziness which must absolutely be avoided. The slowing must be interpreted as a shortening of the stride without decrease in cadence. At the extended walk and the extended trot, seek an extension and not a precipitation of strides; *watch over the regularity of the gait*. The extended trot should be done at the sitting trot as soon as the reactions of the horse, through acquired suppleness, have become soft enough to allow the rider a fixed seat, which is difficult with some horses which have hard gaits.

THE REIN-BACK

There is no use in beginning the rein-back too early, and, in any case, never before having obtained a complete submission to the action of both legs, for it could then become a means of stubborn resistance. This is why it must not be started before this period.

Proceed in the following manner:

1. Position of 1st degree collection as for any movement; the horse is then ready to listen to his rider.

2. Light action of the legs, as if to push the horse forward (in other words, 2nd degree collection but, instead of letting this impulsion escape forward, capture it by resisting with the hand and, at the same time, yielding (descent) of the legs.

3. As soon as the rein-back has begun, the hands must act alternately, each hand acting when the foreleg on the same side is raised to be brought back to the rear. (Base this on the movement of the shoulder.)

4. Legs close to the horse, to watch over the direction of the rein-back and thus forming a sort of corridor in which the horse moves.

If the horse is not straight in his rein-back, use the *indirect rein of opposition, 4th effect*, which will bring back the shoulders in front of the haunches, and do not use isolated leg aids, which would result in putting the haunches behind the shoulders.

Very important. Avoid reining the horse back for too long a time and, above all, vary the number of steps of the rein-back. In fact, the horse *must* always be ready to move forward at the signal of both legs, so that the rein-back does not become a defence.

To stop the rein-back and move the horse forward again: the simultaneous action of both legs must take place at the instant the horse begins a step back. While he is making this step, he has the time to prepare his forward movement.

DIFFICULTIES ENCOUNTERED

Some horses become contracted and refuse to move backwards. In order to overcome this difficulty, above all, do not increase the action of the hands. The resistance would increase and the horse would often prefer to rear up rather than to step back. The answer is obtain mobility of the haunches, which are necessarily the seat of resistance. Nothing is simpler: with an isolated leg action, the rider demands a slight displacement of the haunches to the right or to the left, and he takes advantage of this displacement to bring into action his hands for the rein-back. Actually, during this displacement of the haunches, the hindquarters cannot use a point of thrust, and, consequently, the resistance is practically nullified. Thus, this is the favourable moment to demand the movement to the rear.

POSITION OF THE HEAD AND NECK

In order to make the rein-back easier during the first lessons, over-weighting the hindquarters must avoided. Thus, it is indispensable to place the horse with his neck a little low rather than too high. If the rein-back is demanded on too high a neck, the difficulty will be increased, and the rider risks pushing the horse into a halt with stiff hindlegs and, in persisting, even forcing him to rear up. It is quite evident that when the horse is trained, the rein-back is demanded in the normal position of the 2nd degree collection.

With horses manifesting too great difficulties, which is very rare if the rider is skilful, the rein-back can be started from the dismounted position, the trainer standing in front of the horse. Take care to start by lowering the neck by bringing pressure from above to below on the snaffle, then drawing from front to rear. Be satisfied with one step and then stroke the horse.

WORK PROGRAMME A

1. *Combined Effect:*
   At the halt and the walk
2. *Work on two tracks:*
   Counter changes of hand at the walk (from the track as far as the centre point and then return to the track.)
   At the trot — half-pass.
3. *Shoulder-in:*
   At the walk and trot.
4. *Turns on the forehand:*
   Half turns on the forehand on an inside track.
5. *Canter (true):*
   Slowing on progressively smaller circles and on the straight line.
6. *Counter canter:*
   On circles, progressively decreasing the diameter according to progress.
7. *Transitions:*
   Special attention to the slow walk, the extended walk, the extended walk, slow trot and extended trot.
   Begin rein-back.

WORK PROGRAMME B

1. *Combined effect:*
   At the halt, the walk, and the trot.
2. *Work on two tracks:*

Counter changes of hand at the walk and the trot.

3. *Shoulder-in:*[5]
At the walk and the trot.

4. *Turns (pirouettes):*
Half turns on the forehand. Begin half turns on the haunches.

5. *Canter:*
Special attention to the slow canter on the straight line and to the counter canter. Canter departs on the circle from the slow trot.

6. *Transitions:* Same as Work Programme A.

WORK PROGRAMME C

1. *Combined effect:*
At the halt, the walk, and the trot.

2. *Work on two tracks:*
At the walk and the trot. Counter changes of hand.
At the walk. Tail to the wall, cross the riding hall on two tracks and end with head to the wall.

3. *Turns (Pirouettes):*
Balance the horse between a half turn on the forehand to the right and one to the left.
Half-turns on the haunches. Tighten the circle described by the hind-legs.

4. *Canter:*
Seek to slow the canter more and more.
Improve the counter canter.
Canter departs on the straight line from the slow trot.
Canter departs on the circle from the walk.

5. *Transitions:*
As for Work Programme B and balance the horse between four or five steps of rein back and four or five steps forward.

---

[5] Reference will no longer be made to the shoulder-in. This should be continued.

WORK PROGRAMME D

1. *Combined Effect:*
   At the halt, the walk, and the trot.
2. *Work on two tracks:*
   At the walk and the trot. Counter changes of hand.
   At the trot. Work done at the walk in Work Programme C.
   At the walk. Work on two tracks as in steps of the staircase (a few steps of half-pass, go straight, a few steps of half-pass, and so on).
3. *Turns* Without change for:
   Half turns on the forehand.
   Half turns on the haunches. Try to pivot almost in place.
4. *Canter:*
   Slow canter and counter canter.
   Canter departs on the straight line from the trot and the walk.
5. *Transitions* (without change)

WORK PROGRAMME E

1. *Combined Effect:* (without change)
2. *Work on two tracks:*
   At the walk (without change)
   At the trot. The work done at the walk in Work Programme D.
   At the canter. On the diagonal from the half-circle.
3. *Turns* (without change)
4. *Canter:*
   Slowed canter and serpentines without changing lead.
   Canter departs on the straight line, true and counter canter.[6]

---

[6] Be satisfied with a few good departs — the tendency is always to demand too much.

5. *Transitions* (without change).

WORK PROGRAMME F

1. *Combined Effect:* (without change)
2. *Work on two tracks:*
   At the walk and the trot. Successive counter changes
   of hand (eight strides in each direction).
   At the canter. On the diagonal.
3. *Turns*
   Complete turns on the forehand and complete turns
   on the haunches.
4. *Canter:*
   Serpentines without changing leads and figure eight.
   Canter departs. Counter canter on the circle.
5. *Transitions:* (without change)
   Rein-back. Try to balance the horse between two or
   three steps at the rein-back and two or three steps
   forward.

PART VI

THE FOURTH PERIOD

The principal goal of the Fourth Period will be to perfect all the movements already learned, and it will also include the following:

1. Half halt.
2. Canter departs from the halt.
3. Changes of lead at the canter.
4. Combined effect at the canter.
5. Extended trot.
6. Halts with the combined effect.

At the present stage of training, the work at the walk and the trot should be done correctly and should be nearing perfection.

Now is the time to pay particular attention to the canter.

WORK ON TWO TRACKS

At the walk and the trot, perfect all the movements done in the preceding periods and increase the difficulty in the closely linked counter changes of hand by decreasing the number of strides in each direction (a maximum of six strides). These movements must not only be executed correctly, but the rider must also try to increase the amplitude of the crossing of the legs, as well as suppleness in execution.

However, when the maximum of amplitude has been obtained, it is necessary in the counter changes of hand, to decrease the size of the stride which precedes the change of direction, so that the movement may be performed with ease and suppleness.

The horse may also be worked on the 'herringbone' figure, by pivoting successively from a right angle after a few strides of half-pass from one direction to the other. In this way are obtained a succession of half-passes to the right and to the left executed in the same direction.

The pivoting is done either around the forehand (one quarter turn on the forehand) or around the haunches (one quarter turn on the haunches).

All this work will result in a progressively greater submission, and, consequently, the preponderance of the isolated leg will decrease and will become a simple indication. The preponderance will then pass to the other leg whose goal is to maintain the forward movement through action at the girth. The isolated leg will become preponderant again only in case of the horse's laziness.

At the canter, alternate half-passes and sections of straight lines. This exercise gives brightness and determination to the horse and, at the same time, forces the rider to have more precision in his aids. Take care to engage the shoulders first in each new half-pass.

SHOULDER-IN
As in the Third Period, execution progressively nearer perfection, that is, a correct curving of the entire spinal column, ease and suppleness in execution.

TURNS ON THE FOREHAND
In the turn on the forehand, try to have the crossing-over of the hindlegs as great as possible, at the same time, avoiding a moment of halt which happens at the end of each crossing-over when the horse is insufficiently confirmed. However, with the idea of doing away with this moment of halt, which is ungraceful, do not precipitate the movement. On the contrary, seek a slow, ample, continuous and supple movement. In this way, all the grace indispensable to the perfect execution of a turn on the forehand will be obtained.

TURNS ON THE HAUNCHES
Seek a greater mobility of the hindlegs. The hind pivot must position itself in the same place during the entire turn. Nevertheless, it is preferable that this foot describe a very small circle rather than step back.

The obedience to the isolated leg can be perfected by

balancing the horse from one hindleg to the other. This is the 'balancer' of the hindquarters.

A greater mobility of the shoulders can also be obtained by balancing the horse from one foreleg to the other. This is the 'balancer' of the forehand.

The first one is the beginning of the turn on the forehand; the second, a beginning of the turn on the haunches. In the first case, if the displacement towards the right is begun as soon as the right hindleg is put to the ground, the action of the isolated right leg stops the displacement. The left hindleg is then in the air, and the action of the right leg, after having stopped the displacement of the hindquarters, sends them towards the left, as if to make them begin a turn on the forehand to the left, which, in turn, is stopped by the isolated left leg as soon as the left hindleg is put to the ground. The rider thus attains a balancing of the horse from one hindleg to the other, the neck and the head remaining in the axis of the horse.

This movement makes the horse very attentive to the legs aids, which, for this reason, must be very precise.

In the second case, if a displacement is begun towards the right, as soon as the right foreleg is put to the ground, the forehand is stopped by the right bearing rein; the left foreleg is then in the air.

This rein continues its action, and the forehand is carried towards the left and stopped by the left bearing rein when the left foreleg is put to the ground. A great mobility of the forehand will thus be obtained, but the horse must be very light to the hand and perfectly obedient to the bearing rein.

These two balancer exercises are not indispensable to obtain brilliant execution in the work on two tracks. They are pointed out as an indication to those who wish to acquire great refinement and a greater precision in the isolated leg action.

The half-halt, which was mentioned in regard to the resistances of weight, has the objective of placing the weight on the hindquarters without backing the horse into a halt with stiff hindlegs. Its use prevents the horse from putting too much weight forward and being heavy on the hand. It also makes possible a progressive elevation of the neck.

It is permissible to use the half-halt earlier in training, but it must not be used too freely, and it really becomes helpful only at this period of training.

The half-halt does not consist of jerks, as is frequently seen and as is described even by some so-called qualified riders. It must not be confused with the half-halts used in jumping. In fact, these half-halts, in order to be effective at the right time and, at the same time, act upon the body weight of the horse and the speed, must be carried out rapidly and nearly always forcefully and often brutally.

In dressage training, the half-halt has a different meaning and is performed in the following manner:

Raise the hands quite slowly and vertically, fingernails on top, tightening the fingers on the reins. This gesture must give the impression of lifting a heavy weight. As soon as the horse yields in his mouth, immediate surrender of hands (descent of hands). This also can be done with one rein.

The half-halt in this manner must not modify the speed nor gait, and, if at the halt, it must not cause a rein-back. This expression 'half-halt' has been consecrated by custom, but it only conveys imperfectly the idea which it represents, since, in itself, it means a slowing; whereas, it is actually only a transfer of weight from the front to the rear.

CANTER (SLOWING AND EXTENDING)

The slowing at the canter carried out up to now has prepared the horse for the 'slow canter'. In order to obtain this the horse must be extremely light, a sign of perfect balance, which he must have to maintain this gait with ease. This lightness is obtained by putting weight on the hindquarters, hence the necessity of soft and repeated half-halts, if this is necessary. Since this work is very tiring for the horse, especially at first, demand only a few slow strides followed by a few strides of medium canter, alternating slow canter and medium canter.

Parallel to seeking a maximum slowing, it becomes necessary to demand greater extensions. Up to now, the extensions have hardly exceeded the normal canter, due to the fact that the rider had, first of all, to remain master of the equilibrium. As training progresses, the variations of speed at the canter should become more marked, progressively leading up to transition from slow canter to the most extended canter possible without the right ceasing to be master of the equilibrium.

The transition between the two extreme speeds should be done rapidly, yet maintaining a certain amount of progressiveness. Any harsh or abrupt change in speed must be avoided. The maximum speed desired must come only after a few strides, which makes it possible, along with a rapid transition, to keep the harmony indispensable to correct performance.

As for any extension of gait, it is necessary to allow a light extension of the neck, but this must not alter the lightness. In this case, any preponderance of weight on the shoulders is contended with by half-halts.

If the horse remains light and therefore, balanced, it will be easy to go from extension to slowing. The degree of extension is, thus, in function to the preservation of lightness at this gait.

To avoid changes of lead, keep the bend in the extension, and watch over the haunches with the outside leg.

2ND DEGREE COLLECTION

Before going on to the canter depart from the halt, 2nd degree collection must be improved, and this has already been prepared by the transitions.

At the halt, with the horse in 1st degree collection, by a light and alternate action of the legs, try to put him into a half-impulsion by stimulating the hindlegs, in order to make them ready to go into action at the slightest demand of the rider. Actually, it is indispensable not to create too strong an opposition between the hands and the legs, which is bound to happen with too energetic an action of both legs, since the horse responds normally to this action by moving forward.

This forward movement would be stopped too harshly by the hands, while the rider would only be seeking a 2nd degree collection at the halt. There is no need to fear this disadvantage when the horse is moving, for the action of both legs is expressed by an increase in impulsion, but this impulsion, instead of being expressed by an increase in speed, can be caught by the hands, without a brutal shock, due to the very fact that the horse is moving. Nevertheless, it is, of course, necessary, to proportion the leg action, which must be as energetic as for a transition.

HORSE NOT CANTERING STRAIGHT

As was stated in the third period, this fault is corrected by placing the shoulders before the haunches by means of the rein of indirect opposition 4th effect.

The lighter the horse, the weaker will be this rein effect, and, consequently, the less it will oppose the *placer*, which is inevitably more or less destroyed during the time of its action.

CANTER DEPARTS FROM THE HALT

With the horse in 2nd degree collection, the canter depart will be demanded in the following manner:

1. Give the position corresponding to the lead on which one wishes to canter. For the canter to the right, 'bend' to the right, and light indication of isolated left leg.

2. Give impulsion, either with both legs equal, if the horse is sufficiently confirmed to obey without hesitation the action of the hand on the side of the *placer*, or with a slight preponderance of the outside leg (left leg for the canter to the right), in order to avoid confusing the horse, as long as his reflexes are not entirely confirmed.

3. With impulsion assured, indication of the hand of the bend. So that the depart will not be abrupt, in the first lessons, allow one or two strides at the walk between the halt and the canter, but, soon after, a canter depart should be obtained with no intermediate stride at the walk.

After a few strides at the canter, return to the walk and then to the halt, and then demand the depart on the same side several times in a row. Start with the side which seems to be the easier; the other side will be given particular attention later. Be satisfied with a few good departs on each lead during each lesson.

DEPARTS AT CLOSE INTERVALS

As soon as the horse takes the canter without hesitation, from the trot as well as from the walk and the halt, and he goes lightly at the slow canter, he is ready to begin departs at close intervals.

In this work, the rider must try to maintain the same lightness permanently; in other words, this work must be done in a good 2nd degree collection. The instant the horse leaves this state, bring him back to it before continuing and proceed in the following manner:

1. Canter depart from the trot, the walk, or the halt.
2. A few strides at the canter.
3. Return to the trot, the walk, or the halt.
4. Now depart on the other lead; after a few strides at the trot, the walk, or from the halt. The halt must be as

short as possible without neglecting the 2nd degree collection[1].

CHANGES OF LEAD

Changes of lead may be begun as soon as departs at close intervals are done easily and correctly, with a simple time of halt between two successive departs.

The first changes of lead will be demanded at the end of a half-circle or at the end of a diagonal. To simplify this work, the rider's demand must be made at the precise instant when the horse returns to the track.

When at the canter on the right lead:

1. Change the bend and left bearing rein to straighten the horse and put him in the position favourable to the canter to the left.

2. Reverse the leg action, and, as in the beginning of the demands for canter departs, be sure to have clear and precise aids without forgetting the change of seat.

3. At the same time, action of the left hand, same action as for the canter departs, that is, successive tightening of the fingers with successive elevations of the hand, tightening and elevations effected simultaneously. Wait for the change of lead to happen. It is evident that, as long as the reflexes are not educated, there will be hesitation on the part of the horse, which will not immediately understand

---

[1] It is a good idea not to systematically demand alternate departs to the right and the left. Routine must be avoided and the horse must be kept awake. To accomplish this, vary the demands as much as possible (2 or 3 departs on one lead and one on the other, for example). The horse must obey the rider's demands and not mechanically perform a well-learned lesson. In addition, it is necessary not to work solely on the track of the riding school; these departs must also be demanded on an inner track, at about one metre from the wall, making sure that the horse is perfectly straight.

this new demand. In other words, a new language must be established between the rider and the horse. As long as this language is not familiar to the horse, there will be no instantaneous action. Most of the time, it will only be after several successive demands, following a change in position and equilibrium given to the horse, that he will decide to carry out the change of lead, but, if the rider rewards instantantly, this hesitation will quickly disappear.

With a trained horse, the action of the hand alone is enough to cause a change of lead. At the present time, it is a question of successive actions, because the horse must understand and his reflexes must be educated. The result is that the leg action and, in particular, that of the isolated leg must be clear and sufficiently energetic, even if this causes a slightly oblique movement. Above all, a change of lead must be brought about. As soon as it is obtained, surrender of hands and legs (descent), and pat the horse to show clearly that this was the rider's wish. It is even a good idea to dismount and send the horse back to the stable if he has shown any difficulty.

As for any movement, begin with the side which seems easier. To do this, canter on the lead which the horse likes less; since he prefers to canter on the other lead, he will be all the more willing to change. Later, the other lead will be given special attention.

If, in spite of a correct demand, the horse does not obey after several actions of the hand, bring him back to a state of calm because he will inevitably be nervous. Then begin again with more energetic aids. When the horse has reached this stage of training, if the rider is precise, the change of lead should come about. If not, this means that the preparation in insufficient and then it is necessary to return to departs at close intervals.

Especially avoid making the horse nervous; with each new difficulty, the question of calm becomes of prime importance. Thus, if the horse is too nervous, it is better to stop the lesson and take it up again later. Nervousness does not come from unwillingness, but from lack of understanding. Afterwards, ask for only a few changes of lead at a time. There is always a tendency to demand too much. Progress will be felt not by the number of changes of lead performed, but by seeking a progressively more correct way of doing them.

From the very beginning, it is important to be sure that the change of lead is not being done by the forehand only, but that it is started by the hindquarters (hindleg corresponding to the first phase).

The steps to follow are:

1. Change of lead at the end of the half-circle or the diagonal.
2. Change of lead on the circle from the counter canter.
3. Change of lead on the straight line.
4. Change of lead on the circle from the true canter.[2]

WHEN SHOULD THE CHANGE BE DEMANDED?

It is obvious that the change of lead should not be demanded at just any phase of the canter stride. There is a time when it is easier for the horse to carry it out. This instant must be seized, if immediate action is desired, and this will be very important when close successive changes of lead are reached.

The third phase of the canter is the most favourable, because, at this time, only one foreleg is grounded, while the other three legs are in the air. Thus, they are in a favourable situation to be prepared to modify the succession of footfalls, and the following phase, which is the phase of suspension, will allow the horse to prepare his new stride.

---

[2] The action of the hand which is used to demand either the canter depart or the change of lead must be given with an upward motion and must not be confused with the action of the indirect rein.

Taking into account the fraction of a second necessary for the rider's indications to be transmitted to the horse's leg through the intermediary of the horse's brain, the rider's demand should be made slightly before the third phase.

The result is that the rider should develop an instinctive feeling for the footfalls, so that he may act with precision and at the right moment in the very short time which is the favourable instant to demand of the horse the change of lead.

COMBINED EFFECT

To be improved at the walk and the trot, and to be begun at the canter. Same principles for all three gaits; there should be no modifications in the gait.

SLOW WALK AND TROT

In the slow walk and the slow trot, work on elevation of the neck by means of half-halts followed by surrender of the hands (descent). At first, the horse must remain in the position given him for a few instants without help from the hands, *maintaining himself on his own*. Little by little, this carriage should last as long as the rider desires. As soon as the horse gives up the position, do another half-halt.

The maximum elevation of the neck depends upon the horse's conformation. The same elevation cannot be required of all horses without disadvantages, but, in all cases, a fairly high neck position must be obtained.

EXTENDED WALK

Continue to work on the extended walk during the whole training period. If necessary, push with the seat. Do not forget to demand a few strides of extended walk before each rest period.

EXTENDED TROT (Dressage or School gait)

As a rule, this should be done at the sitting trot. The

extended trot (school gait) is nothing other than the extended trot pushed to the maximum of extension with pursuit of a slower cadence.

At the end of the preceding period, the extended trot should have been regular, that is, equal strides and same engagement of both hindlegs. Now, it is a question of seeking the maximum extension without precipitating the cadence and this during a few strides only in the first lessons.

MEANS TO BE USED

1. Seek lightness, for, although a little more marked contact with a slight extension of the neck is admissable, nevertheless, the horse must not weight upon the hand; this would prove that the balance has been changed. Now, in order to obtain a brilliant, supple, and graceful extended trot (dressage or school gait), the horse must be master of his equilibrium and, at no time, should the forehand be over-weighted.

2. With the horse at a regular extended trot (*au trot allongé*) try to obtain a greater extension by placing the weight slightly more on the shoulder of the diagonal that is grounded by action of the bearing rein (left rein when the right diagonal is grounded).

This action of the hand must take place when the diagonal on the same side (left diagonal for the left bearing rein) is lifted. It should be done with accuracy and correct timing, so as not to stop the extension, which is bound to happen if this action is prolonged.

3. Legs equal, active, and even energetic, if necessary.

Some horses will not do an extended trot (dressage gait) unless the legs are really energetic and strong.[3]

---

[3]The extended trot (dressage or school gait) can also be demanded with the action of the direct rein or opposition, on the same side as the foreleg which is grounded, but a more brilliant effect is obtained with the first action. This second action is to be used preferably with a horse which lacks lightness, the other action requires a horse that is light.

HALTS

Up to now, halts have been demanded in a more or less progressive manner, with one, or several, strides of intermediary gaits. Now that the horse is trained to the combined effect, the halts must be done without passing through an intermediate gait. Thus, they should be instantaneous without being abrupt nor ungraceful. They should be demanded in the following manner:

1. A few strides before the halt, whatever the gait, canter trot, or walk. Slow the horse slightly while maintaining activity of the hindlegs.

2. Combined effect.

3. Along with the combined effect, action of both hands to demand the halt.

4. As soon as the horse is immobile, surrender (descent) of hands and legs.

This procedure makes it possible to 'set' the halt and to immediately obtain a motionless state.

Especially at the canter, it is necessary to have two or three strides of very slow canter to obtain an excellent, though not brutal, halt followed by complete immobility.

REIN-BACK

Perfection of the rein-back consists of:

1. The horse backing calmly and slowly with strides as long as possible.

2. The horse always ready to move forward at the lightest indication of the legs. In order to have a calm horse, the rider must be calm himself, and he must not have harsh nor jerky action. In other words, he must have a 'gallant hand'. In addition, demand little at a time.

In order to keep the horse awake and ready to move forward, balance him between a few steps of rein-back and a few stops forward. At first, two steps of rein-back and two steps forward.

As soon as he is sufficiently obedient in this work,

balance him between one step of rein-back and one step forward. This exercise demands a great deal of accuracy on the part of the rider, because the movement must be done without a moment of halt. Work both sides equally. To begin a rein-back on the right lead, for example, action of the isolated right leg and action of left direct rein of opposition. In fact, the action of the right leg will cause the right hindleg to be raised as if to move forward and the action of the left direct rein, which must be only slightly preponderant, with the neck remaining straight, will force this hindleg to move behind the left one. Great precision in the aids is indispensable, but this exercise makes the horse particularly attentive and obedient.

WORK PROGRAMME A

1. *Work on two tracks:*
   At the walk and the trot, counter changes of hand of six strides. At the canter — half-pass as far as the centre line, go straight for a few strides and then half-pass again in the same direction.
2. *Turns on the haunches and on the forehand:*
   Without change. Work on the mobility of the hindlegs on the haunches.
3. *Combined effect:*
   Begin this at a rather slow canter.
4. *Canter:*
   Slow canter, from the extended canter.
   Canter depart from the halt (work on 2nd degree collection).
   Departs at close intervals from the trot and the walk.
5. *Transitions:*
   Extended trot (dressage gait) for a few strides.
   Rein-back. Balance with one or two strides.
   Extended walk; continue to improve.
   Halts: work on the combined effect at the halt, starting from the walk and the trot.

WORK PROGRAMME B

1. *Work on two tracks:*
   At the walk and the trot (without change).
   At the canter. Work as in steps of the staircase (a few steps of half-pass, go straight, a few steps of half-pass, and so on).
2. *Turns on the haunches and turns on the forehand:* (without change) 'Balancer' of the forehand and the hindquarters.
3. *Combined effect:* At all three gaits.
   Use it to demand halts.
4. *Canter:*
   Canter departs from the halt.
   Departs at close intervals (without change).
   Isolate changes of lead at the end of a half volte.
5. *Transitions:*
   Rein-back from the walk, with practically no time at the halt.
   Halts. Work on halts with combined effect, starting from the canter.
   The rest without change.

WORK PROGRAMME C

1. *Work on two tracks:*
   Add — at the canter, work with haunches-in on the circle to prepare the pirouette.
2. *Turn on the haunches and turn on the forehand* (without change).
3. *Combined effect* (without change).
4. *Canter:*
   Departs at close intervals starting from the halt.
   Single changes of lead on the circle starting from the counter canter.
5. *Transitions:*
   Increase the number of strides of the extended trot (dressage gait). The rest without change.

WORK PROGRAMME D

1. *Work on two tracks:*
   At the walk and trot, herringbone.
   At the canter, work with the haunches-in on the circle.
   Half-pass on the diagonal.
2. *Turns on the haunches and turns on the forehand:*
   (without change).
3. *Combined effect.*
   Without change — reference will no longer be made to
   this: to be perfected up to the end of training.
4. *Canter:*
   Departs at close intervals.
   Changes of lead on the straight line.
5. *Transitions* (without change).

WORK PROGRAMME E

1. *Work on two tracks:* At the canter.
   Decrease the diameter of the inner circle.
   The rest without change.
2. *Turns on the haunches and turns on the forehand:*
   (without change).
3. *Canter:*
   Departs at close intervals.
   Isolated changes of lead on the straight line and on
   the circle starting from the true canter.
4. *Transitions*
   Extended trot (dressage gait) for the whole length of
   the riding school and on the diagonal.
   Halts on the combined effect from the canter.[4]

---

[4] It is evident that these new exercises must not cause those already
discussed to be forgotten and that it is necessary to return frequently
to everything important.

PART VII

THE FIFTH PERIOD

This, the Fifth, Period will be especially concerned with refining the movements studied in the preceding periods, and, in particular, those which the horse does not yet perform correctly.

The rider should be very demanding, and he should seek perfection in all of his work, following the principles already stated. It would be preferable for him to mark time during the training process until he has obtained satisfaction in all the movements, namely:

1. Correct *placer*.
2. Calm horse with maximum impulsion.
3. Perfect equilibrium and lightness.

In addition, this period will include:

   a) *Work on two tracks:*

     — Counter changes of hand at the canter.

   b) *Canter:*

     — Canter departs from the rein-back.

     — Changes of lead at close intervals.

     — Preparation for the pirouette at the canter.

WORK ON TWO TRACKS

AT THE WALK AND THE TROT

Continue to improve this, taking inspiration from the advice already given. In addition, when the movement is started, a well-schooled horse should move on the half-pass by pushing solely on the rein which gives the bend, while the other rein remains lightly stretched in contact with the neck. The action of the isolated leg is no longer preponderant. Equal action of both legs is sufficient, and, with some horses, the direct leg even becomes preponderant, with the isolated leg being kept ready to act. It follows that the horse remains perfectly in the forward movement, absolute condition for a good half-pass, and in an impeccable *placer* during the entire performance of the movement.

Counter change in hand with change of lead. As at the walk and the trot, the forehand must precede the hindquarters. The result of this is that the horse moves on a slightly diagonal line, a position which is favourable to the change of lead.

Avoid surprising the horse, which would result in an abrupt change of lead. The preparation for the change of direction, with a change of lead, is carried out by decreasing the amplitude of the last two strides. Then, warn the horse by changing the bend and, at the time of the change of lead, straighten him by a light action of the rein of indirect opposition, 4th effect, so that he may be enabled to take the new direction.

For example, for a counter change of hand from right to left, change of lead from right to left, and immediately afterwards, right indirect rein of opposition 4th effect, which will straighten the horse and engage the shoulders in the new direction.

At first, in order to keep the horse calm, leave him on the straight line for one or two strides before starting the new half-pass. In this work, calm can be maintained only by avoiding any kind of surprise to the horse, which may be resumed for the rider as *placer and precision*.

TURNS ON THE FOREHAND AND HAUNCHES

Seek:

Maximum of amplitude in the crossing of the legs (hindlegs for the turn on the forehand and forelegs for the turn on the haunches.)

Great mobility of the hindlegs in the turn on the haunches while trying to position the pivot leg in the same place each time.

Continuity of the movement and suppleness in the crossing. Actually, the steps must follow each other without stopping after each crossing.

COMBINED EFFECT
Work on this with special thought given to halts.

TRANSITIONS
In the slow walk and the slow trot, seek the following:
— Slow to maximum with strong action of the hindlegs.
— Great lightness with the neck as high as possible.

In order to avoid fatigue, alternate the slow walk with the medium walk, and the slow trot with the medium trot.

EXTENDED TROT (Dressage gait)
Seek the maximum extension and *regularity*.

Try to decrease the cadence, while avoiding a trot which resembles the Spanish trot, that is, with an exaggerated elevation of the forelegs.

EXTENDED CANTER AND SLOW CANTER
Seek:
— Lightness, in the extended canter as well as in the slow canter.
— Rapid and supple transitions.
— Particular attention to having the horse straight in the extension where the horse has a tendency to go back to his natural habits.

In the slow canter, take care to avoid a four-beat canter, which inevitably happens when the hindquarters become lazy; thus, the necessity of greater impulsion as the rate becomes slower.

Since this canter is very tiring for the horse, alternate a few strides of slow canter with a few strides of medium canter.

Also work on the slow canter starting from the slow walk in the following manner:

1. Put the horse at a slow walk.

2. Demand the canter depart and maintain the slowed canter for a few strides.

3. With the combined effect, return to the slow walk and repeat this exercise several times. Also do the same work starting from the halt.

3RD DEGREE (highest) COLLECTION

All of these gaits, slow walk, slow trot, and slow canter, are none other than the collected (*rassemble*) walk, trot, and canter when they are performed with perfect lightness and maximum engagement of the hindlegs.

3rd degree collection (*rassembler*) may be defined as *2nd degree collection with engagement of the hindlegs*. Although 2nd degree collection is within the capability of many riders, 3rd degree, on the contrary, can only be obtained by highly skilled riders with particularly refined tact.

In fact, it is indispensable that the impulsion given by the legs, with the goal of engaging the hindquarters, be received by an extremely sensitive hand, which is capable of letting pass through or retaining the quantity of impulsion which will make possible the perfect and instable equilibrium known as 3rd degree collection.

Mobility of the horse's legs with progressive engagement of the hindlegs will make possible a beginning of 3rd degree collection. By frequently demanding this mobility of the horse's legs, the highest degree will be reached and this will result in the piaffer. This proves the importance of doing turns on the haunches with mobility of the hindlegs as described above. It is obtained more easily with a horse of good conformation than with a subject with faulty conformation, such as sickle hocks or cow hocks, a long, weak back, etc. Obviously, the trainer must be less demanding, very methodical and very progressive with such horses if he wants them to remain sound.

In addition, the difficulty consists in keeping 3rd degree collection during the entire execution of the movement, which requires a very precise use of fingers and legs on the part of the rider.

115

Only if the horse is totally straight, perfectly light to the hand and has his neck sufficiently high is 3rd degree collection possible. And it is indispensable in obtaining perfect and brilliant performances of Haute Ecole figures such as the piaffer, passage forwards and backwards, canter in place, pirouettes at the canter and canter backwards.

REIN-BACK

Vary the number of steps at the rein-back and balance the horse between one stride of rein-back and one stride forward.

For a good rein-back, when it immediately follows a forward movement (walk, trot, or canter), the halt must be excellent, the horse light. In addition, the rein-back must immediately follow the halt, with no hesitation whatsoever in between. However, this must not result in precipitation, for it is better to have a slight hesitation than a rushed rein-back.

HALTS

Perfect them by observing the principles given in the Fourth Period.

Seek soft halts on the combined effect, with no harshness whatsoever, the horse evenly balanced on his four legs, light and calm.

In particular, be sure that the hindlegs are in line with each other. If one hindleg remains behind, bring it into place by a trembling of the calf on the same side.

After the halt, upon the surrender (descent) of the hands, the horse should keep his neck high. Descents of hands, while remaining highly perceptible to the horse should become more and more discreet.

CANTER DEPARTS

Perfect canter departs from the trot, the walk, and the halt.

Seek an easy, supple, immediate depart by light action of the aids, the horse remaining very straight.

Departs should now be demanded with equal legs and a light indication of the hand on the side of the bend. They may also be demanded by preponderant action of the inside leg (right leg, right hand for the depart on the right lead), but the other leg must be ready to act in case the horse hesitates in taking the desired lead.

In fact, the canter depart with the inside leg aid now becomes a question of reflex, because the preponderance of the inside leg has only a conventional value. The result is that the horse can avoid its action each time he wishes. Thus, the outside leg must, at each instant, nip in the bud any tendency toward disobedience by forming a wall on its side.

Some masters say that perfectly straight departs are obtained with the inside leg. There is no doubt about this, but the same result can also be obtained with equal action of both legs, and, in my opinion, this procedure has the advantage of superior impulsion with a more energetic thrust of the hindleg which begins the first stride.

However, with the goal of refining the horse's reflexes and making him more and more attentive, it is a good idea to work on the canter depart with the inside leg.

Work on canter departs starting from the rein-back. Demand a depart on the right lead when the right shoulder moves back.

This is the instant when the right diagonal is preparing to be grounded. The result is that the left hindleg is in a favourable position to start the canter to the right.[1]

---

[1] As the horse becomes more submissive, the education of his reflexes is nearer perfect. The rider must then confine himself to the use of progressively more discreet aids, and the action of the hand demanding the depart must remain almost invisible.

CHANGES OF LEAD

Before demanding changes of lead at close intervals, single changes of lead must first be perfected. It would, of course, be absurd to hope that changes of lead at close intervals would be done with ease as long as single changes of lead are not done perfectly; that is, with lightness and the horse perfectly balanced before, during and after the change of lead. In addition, the horse should strike off without hesitation upon the rider's first demand, hence the necessity of having an attentive and not routined horse.

To accomplish this, be sure that the changes of lead are never demanded in the same place. Demand few at a time and reward the horse as soon as a good change of lead is obtained.

It is also a good idea to vary the work by doing changes of lead on a serpentine, sometimes at the true canter, sometimes at the counter canter, as well as on the figure eight.

Seek precision, by setting points in advance: the centre line in the serpentine, the quarter or three-quarter line in the *doubler* (turn at the centre of the long side and cross over to the centre of the opposite long side of the riding school) and varied points on the straight line. The rider should confine himself to demanding the change of lead only at the point he has fixed in advance. He will thus be forced to prepare his horse in time, and this will result in precision not only on the part of the horse, but also of the rider. Both will approach perfection, one in the execution, and the other in the demand.

In summary, the characteristics of a good change of lead are: lightness, precision, straight horse, and amplitude of movement.

CHANGES OF LEAD AT CLOSE INTERVALS

Changes of lead at close intervals should be begun only when single changes of lead are as near perfect as possible.

In order to do this, decide in advance the number of strides between two successive changes of lead. At the beginning, the number will vary between six and four strides, progressively leading up to two strides.

In this work, seek the same degree of lightness and precision as in the single changes of lead. As soon as the horse places his weight on the forehand and becomes heavy to the hand, adjust his equilibrium by half-halts, for the lack of lightness comes from a change in balance which takes place during the performance of the change of lead. This fault must be fought immediately if the rider wishes to have his horse progress rapidly.

A state of calm is also more necessary than ever. Therefore, all causes of nervousness and disorder must be done away with. The rider will avoid this danger if he is precise in his aids, if he is sure to reward the horse often and gives frequent rest periods. The harder and more difficult the work becomes, the more importance should be attached to having a calm horse. The question of a straight horse becomes of primary importance, because the horse must always be in a position to go from one lead to the other.

STEPS TO FOLLOW
1. Changes of lead on the straight line.
2. Changes of lead on the circle.
3. Changes of lead on the figure eight.

IMPROVEMENT OF THE CHANGE OF LEAD
With a horse which is lazy in the hindquarters, the change of lead can be improved by strong action of the seat at the instant the change of lead takes place. This pressure of the seat must be made at the same time as the demand for the change of lead, using the right buttock for the change of lead from right to left and vice versa for the change of lead from left to right.

PREPARING PIROUETTES AT THE CANTER

Before starting pirouettes at the canter, it is essential that the horse be well-schooled at the slow canter, and, to do a correct pirouette, the horse must be trained to canter in place, but it is not necessary to await this stage before beginning the preparation.

Moreoever, the circles at the canter with haunches-in are already a preparatory exercise for the pirouettes, but the actual preparation will be done in the following manner:

1. Begin a pirouette at the walk.

2. During the course of this pirouette, demand a strike-off at the canter following the same principles as for the canter depart, which will mark one stride at the canter.

3. Continue the pirouette at the walk, and, when the horse has become calm and light again, demand another stride at the canter. As training progresses, demand two or three successive strides at the canter, with the horse remaining on the pirouette.

With this procedure, the horse rapidly understands the rider's desire and no force is needed, because there is nothing new for him from the point of view of pirouette and canter depart; all that remains is to combine the canter stride with the displacement of the pirouette. And, in the work at the canter with haunches-in, this combination is already in existence. In addition, this work is not tiring as long as it is a question of only a few strides.

It is evident that the pirouette will be all the easier to do as the horse is confirmed in the slow canter or even the canter in place. Therefore, this movement will be improved by perfecting the slow canter and trying to obtain the canter in place. During this period, only the preparation for the pirouette will be done. Actual pirouettes at the canter will not be started until the next period.

PART VIII

THE SIXTH PERIOD

The Sixth Period will be that of the Haute Ecole proper, and it will include:

1. Counter changes of hand at the canter at close intervals.
2. Changes of lead at each stride.
3. Canter in place.
4. Canter backwards.
5. Passage and piaffer.
6. Pirouettes at the canter.

WORK ON TWO TRACKS

COUNTER CHANGES OF HAND AT THE CANTER AT CLOSE INTERVALS

In the preceding period, the counter change of hand at the canter was a single change of hand. At the beginning, it was demanded with a few strides on the straight line after the change of lead, but these strides must now be done away with progressively and only the change of lead stride must be done on the straight line. The result of this that the diagonal movement, considered favourable to the change of lead, must also disappear when this final stage of training is reached and the horse must be perfectly straight at the time the change of lead is demanded.

In order to execute this movement easily and correctly, as at the walk and the trot, the amplitude of crossing-over of the last stride must be decreased and advantage should be taken of this decrease to straighten the horse by doing away with the advance that the forehand may have on the hindquarters. To do this, the action of the indirect rein (left rein for half-pass toward the right) should be decreased or even done away with and, if necessary, the shoulders may be stopped by a light action of the indirect rein on the side of the bend (right rein in the case given above).

Demand the change of lead at the end of this stride. Since the horse is straight at the time of the change of lead, he will be ready to start the half-pass in the opposite direction. This stride of the change of lead represents the first one of the new half-pass.

At the second stride, take care to start the half-pass with the forehand slightly in advance over the hindquarters. In order to accomplish this, the action of the indirect rein (right rein in the half-pass toward the left) must precede the action of the isolated leg (right leg).

With this procedure, the horse will never be surprised and the counter change of hand will be fluid and graceful.

Decide in advance the number of strides desired on each branch of the counter change of hand. Begin with eight or ten strides eventually to arrive at six, which corresponds to the movement demanded at the Olympic Games.

CHANGES OF LEAD AT EACH STRIDE

The horse which gives changes of lead at close intervals up to that of two strides, without hesitation, with lightness and perfect balance, can take on changes of lead at each stride.

At the beginning, of course, it is out of the question to demand a whole series of changes of lead at each stride. The horse would be surprised by the repeated and rapid demands of the rider, causing a loss of balance and lightness followed by a state of nervousness. This would be poor work, requiring a return to changes of lead at close intervals during a fairly long period.

To avoid this waste of time, follow the steps given below:

1. *Changes of lead 1, 2*

This exercise consists in demanding two successive changes of lead during the course of two successive strides of canter. In this way, a change of lead at each stride will be obtained.

For example, while at the canter on the right lead, perform a change of lead from right to left, followed, at

123

the next stride by a change of lead from left to right. Thus, a change of lead at each stride will have been obtained, only one, because the first one was actually an ordinary change of lead.

At first, this exercise must always be demanded from a depart on the same lead. Then, when the horse has understood, take up the same exercise with depart on the other lead. In this way, the horse will know how to execute a change of lead at each stride on both sides.

2. *Changes of lead 1, 2, 3*

Instead of two successive changes of lead, this time, three are demanded, sometimes starting from the canter to the right and sometimes from the canter to the left. In this way, two changes of lead at each stride will have been obtained, and the horse will end up on the opposite lead from the one where he started.

3. *Changes of lead 1, 2, 3, 4*

When the preceding exercise no longer presents any difficulties, four successive changes of lead are demanded. Thus, three changes of lead at each stride are obtained, and the horse ends up on the lead he started with.

Do not forget to work on both leads. That is, sometimes begin with the canter to the right and sometimes to the left.

When this exercise is performed correctly, the horse may be considered to be trained to changes of lead at each stride. Now, only the number of these changes needs to be increased.

For the rider, the difficulty consists in never being behind the horse's cadence. It is indispensable that the change of 'bend', which must be slight, and the demand for change of lead, be made almost instantaneously. This is a question of skill and precision on the part of the rider.

At the beginning, so as to make changes in seat easier, the rider may place the upper part of his body slightly forward, but, afterwards, for a harmonious rider-horse combination, the rider should make an effort to maintain the normal position. In other words, sit deeply in the saddle with the upper part of the body perfectly straight.

CANTER IN PLACE

Canter in place is obtained progressively by a more marked shortening of the canter, which makes it necessary to have the horse in maximum impulsion to maintain action of the hindlegs and to avoid a four-beat canter. Therefore, the rider must have active legs and carefully regulate the alternate actions of his hands. The leg action must also be alternate, and the rider should have practiced this in the canter with 3rd degree collection.

When the canter 3rd degree collection covers less and less ground, the rider resists more with his fingers, so as to obtain one or two strides of canter in place, but a great precision in the aids is necessary. On the one hand, a great deal of impulsion must be maintained and, on the other hand, the action of the hands must be measured exactly to maintain the canter mechanism while at the same time remaining in place. Perfect balance and lightness are required.

After having obtained one or two strides of canter in place, move forward at the canter 3rd degree colleciton to prevent the canter sequence from stopping. Progressively increase the number of strides of canter in place.

Preparation for the canter in place may also be made at the halt. First, demand mobility of all four feet. Then, with this mobility, demand one stride of canter, return to the halt with mobility of all four feet and do another canter stride on the other lead. When the horse has been gymnastically prepared by this exercise, two strides of canter, instead of one, are demanded and then three and four. In this way, the canter in place is obtained, on condition that work has been done at the same time on the highly collected canter to develop the suppleness and elasticity of the horse necessary for this canter.

CANTER BACKWARDS

When the canter in place is given correctly, the canter backwards may be tried, taking care to be satisfied with little.

To obtain the canter backwards, starting from the canter in place, resist more with the fingers. The seat should be placed slightly back to help the raising of the forehand. In addition, it should move alternately to the right and the left, so as to unweight the left and right hindlegs at the moment they move back. At first, demand only one or two strides. Then return to the canter in place and to the collected canter so that the horse continues to keep the reflex of forward movement.

This work is very hard on the horse, so do not be too demanding. In addition, to maintain the canter sequence, it is indispensable that the canter to the rear be not too fast and not gain more than a few centimetres of ground at each stride; for, in this case, the horse would do a sort of 'crow hop' with his hindlegs, which would have no resemblance whatsoever with the canter backwards.

Do not forget that the rein-back must be straight. If the horse moves back on a diagonal line, put the shoulders before the haunches as in the normal canter by action of the rein of indirect opposition 4th effect.

PASSAGE AND PIAFFER

The passage is a cadenced gait, derived from the trot, which is also executed by successive footfalls of each diagonal. The cadence is slower than that of the trot; the horse covers less ground and gains in height that which he loses horizontally. The legs which are raised mark a slight pause, the forearm nears the horizontal, the canon is vertical and the foot lightly flexed. The whole foreleg then performs a harmonious and graceful movement. The elevation of the hindlegs must be less than that of the forelegs.

Beautiful passage is distinguished by great elevation of the forearm, with no tension whatsoever of the leg and also by a more marked elevation of the hindlegs. In addition, there must be no lateral swinging or balancing.

The piaffer is none other than the passage in place, but the elevation of the legs is a little less marked. The greatest regularity in the rhythm of the legs is indispensable in the piaffer as well as in the passage.

The passage can be obtained in different ways:

1. Starting from the piaffer.

2. Starting from the cadenced trot.

3. By performing highly collected counter changes of hand at close intervals.

This last method must not be used, because it gives the horse a lateral swing which is considered a serious fault and which, in addition, is ungraceful. Some trainers demand the passage from the Spanish Trot, which is an error, because a true and beautiful passage is never obtained with this procedure. In fact, the horse takes the habit of marking an extension of the forelegs, which prevents the canon from remaining vertical.

The piaffer can be obtained by the following methods:

1. By slowing the walk with increased activity of the hindlegs.

2. By slowing the trot.

3. By slowing the passage.

The most rational method of teaching a horse the passage consists of first training the horse to the piaffer and then going from the piaffer to the passage. However, a beautiful passage can be obtained from a horse which has never learned the piaffer. All depends upon the goal which one has set, but, in this case, the training of the horse is incomplete.

WHEN TO BEGIN TRAINING?

The training of the piaffer may be started as soon as the

127

horse is entirely submissive at the walk and the trot; that is, when the transitions at the walk and the trot are performed in perfect 2nd degree collection and with no alteration whatsoever of lightness, which may be situated at the beginning of the Fourth Period.[1]

PREPARATION OF THE PIAFFER

This preparation will be done at the walk and the trot.

WORK AT THE WALK

1. Seek very active hindquarters at a very slow walk, so as to decrease the amount of time which passes between the grounding of the foreleg and that of the hindleg of the same diagonal, because, in the piaffer, the grounding of these two legs must be simultaneous and shorten the walk to the point of obtaining one stride of walk in place, then immediately move forward.

2. At the same time, work on the following movements:

a) Half-turn on the haunches (half pirouette) without crossing of the forelegs, but only a slow lateral displacement with mobility of all four feet.

b) Follow this half-turn on the haunches by a half-turn on the forehand performed under the same conditions as the preceding, that is, mobility of all four feet with a very slow lateral displacement.

c) End with a half-turn on the haunches executed like the first one. Then, rest for a few metres and begin again the same exercise. In this way, work will have been done on each hand.

As training progresses, try to maintain mobility of the legs while in the same place between each half-turn on the haunches during one or two strides.

---

[1] For training of the piaffer and passage, refer to the book, *Piaffer et Passage* by Colonel Decarpentry.

General Rule. After each movement at the walk, halt and demand mobility of all four feet, and then rest with a long rein and then a few strides of extended walk.

WORK AT THE TROT
The variations of gait (transitions) from the walk to the trot, from the halt to the trot and vice versa, have brought the horse to the degree of training which enables him to begin the direct preparation of the piaffer.

It is now a question of balancing the horse in a succession of a few strides of trot interrupted by halts, as short as possible, trying to progressively decrease the number of hoof-beats at the trot and also the length of time at the halt.

The trot will be as slow as possible while remaining cadenced and energetic.

The 2nd degree collection must be perfect, that is, with no alteration whatsoever of lightness and the horse absolutely straight.

As at the walk, end with the forward movement of a few strides of extended trot followed by rest, preferably in place, with long reins.

In all of this work, rigorously observe the principle: 'Hands without legs and legs without hands.'

If the horse becomes lazy, send him forward energetically while yielding with the hands. If, on the contrary, he becomes heavy on the hand, perform a few half-halts while yielding with the legs.

PIAFFER
The preparatory work at the walk and the trot gradually leads to the performance of the piaffer.

AT THE WALK
When mobility of all four feet is easily obtained in place, this is a simili-piaffer, which is not the real piaffer, since

the supporting legs are not yet diagonal; but, by increasing impulsion and, if necessary, allowing the horse to advance a few centimetres at each stride, the association of diagonal supporting legs will be obtained, and, after this, a beginning of piaffer or small piaffer (*petit piaffer*).

AT THE TROT

While maintaining the cadence of the trot, try to decrease the ground covered at each hoof-beat, so as to progressively obtain a trotting stride in place, then two, then three, etc.: this will be the small piaffer.

It is very important to continue to observe the principle 'Hands without legs and legs without hands'.

Do not allow the horse to stop by himself and demand a few strides of strong trot before letting him rest.

In all of this work, try to raise the neck progressively, without modifying lightness. In fact, mobility in place in an equilibrium making possible a correct execution of the piaffer will be reached by raising the neck, but the raising of the neck must not modify the correct form of 1st degree collection.

It is a good idea to alternate a few steps of piaffer in place with a few steps advancing a few centimetres at each stride, so that the cadence will not die out and the horse will always keep the feeling of forward movement. This procedure also has the advantage of avoiding anchoring the hindlegs to the ground and the tendency to do a rein-back. If this happens, send the horse forward without rushing, except in the case where he manifests stubbornness when it is necessary to send him off energetically at an extended trot.

It is very important to be satisfied with little and to reward the horse as soon as three or four well cadenced strides are obtained. In addition, do not forget that the regularity of the gaits is of primary importance.

When the horse has found his balance in the small piaffer, has a supple back, shows no contraction whatsoever and his lightness remains perfect, a higher action should be sought, particularly with the forelegs.

By weighting the foreleg which is grounded, the length of time of its support will be prolonged and this forces the horse to raise the other foreleg in order to keep his balance.

ACTION OF HANDS, SEAT, AND LEGS

The piaffer, like the passage, is a 'hopped' gait, marked by the alternate footfalls of the diagonals with a time of suspension prolonged for the diagonal in suspension. The result is that the horse must remain in equilibrium on the diagonal which is on the ground and the objective of the rider's aids will be to promote, and even to provoke, this equilibrium.

ACTION OF THE HANDS

The objective of the hand is to place the weight on the foreleg which is on the ground and the bearing rein will be in charge of this work. With the right foreleg on the ground, the left bearing rein will be used. At the beginning, of course, be satisfied with a simple closing of the fingers and, little by little, increase the intensity and length of time of the closing of the fingers.

Note that this action can be efficient only if the horse is perfectly in 2nd degree collection.

SEAT

With regard to the hindlegs, the rider's seat must be placed on the side of the hindleg which is on the ground, in order to make possible a more prolonged suspension of the other hindleg and, in certain cases, a simple pressure of the foot on the same side. When the right diagonal is on the ground, the seat should, therefore, be preponderant to the left.

LEGS

The action of the legs should alternate and it should take

place at the moment the hindleg on the same side is going to be on the ground. The leg should not act too soon, so as not to decrease the length of time the horse's leg is on the ground. Thus, the right leg should act at the moment the right diagonal is going to be on the ground. The leg will act more or less behind the girth. However, beware of leg action too far behind the girth, which, with some horses, can result in bringing the hindleg under the body in an exaggerated manner.

It follows from this observation, that, by acting differently with each leg, irregularity which may exist in the hindlegs can be rectified to a certain extent.

WORK FROM THE GROUND

There is no doubt that work from the ground can render great service in the training of the piaffer. However, do not believe that it is indispensable. A skilful and experienced rider can very well obtain a very good piaffer without doing this type of exercise.

With certain lazy horses, dismounted work makes it possible to improve and obtain more rapidly a good piaffer. Naturally, it demands a certain amount of skill on the part of the trainer. It is indispensable to act calmly, avoiding 'spooking' the horse with too sudden gestures. In the work on the ground, confidence is just as necessary as in mounted work. Take a light stick about 1.50 metres long and stand beside the horse, which is placed along the wall of the riding school with the reins placed on his neck. When the horse is on the left hand, the trainer holds the reins in his left hand at 15 centimetres from the mouth; he holds the stick in his right hand.

So as not to frighten the horse, it is necessary to familiarise him with the stick by passing it lightly over his back, croup, thighs and flank, while patting him at the same time. In this way, he will not be afraid of being punished and he will not be frightened at the sight of the stick. Without this precaution, some horses will try to lunge forward at the slightest gesture.

Then, alternately tap the back of each hindleg, at the middle of the canon, until the horse slightly raises his leg. Pat him immediately to make the horse understand that he has done well. In addition, clicking of the tongue should also be associated with the stick, so that the clicking of the tongue alone will mean mobility of the legs and the stick will no longer be used, except to correct laziness. Do not forget to work on both hands and, at the beginning, allow the horse to advance a few centimetres at each foot-fall, so as to always keep him in the forward movement. Then, when he balances himself easily, resist with the hand holding the reins to force the horse to balance himself without advancing.

The next step is to mount the horse and associate the clicking of the tongue and the action of the rider's legs. An assistant now stands on the side and uses the stick at the place indicated each time the horse lacks energy.

Sometimes it is a good idea to use the stick on the inside of the hock to obtain a little more elevation, or to correct an irregularity in the working of the hindlegs.

The riding whip can replace the long stick, by giving little taps on the croup to maintain cadence. The horse being accustomed to this in the work on the ground, once the rider is mounted, he can use it to make the horse understand a leg aid or to reinforce leg action.

When the horse is well trained in work on the ground, the assistant may be dispensed with, but, when mounted work is being done, it is a good idea to do a few minutes of work on the ground at the beginning of each lesson. In this case, the rider stands near the horse's shoulder and holds the reins in his left hand if the horse is on the left rein and in his right hand when the horse is going to the right. He holds the long stick, or preferably the riding whip, in the other hand and he uses it by giving little taps either at the place where the spur normally acts, or on the top of the croup, as described above. Associate the action of the riding whip with the clicking of the tongue.

All of these exercises must be considered only as preparatory work, because the goal is the piaffer under the rider, who uses only his aids with no help whatsoever from the riding whip or clicking of the tongue.

PASSAGE, STARTING FROM THE PIAFFER

Once a correct piaffer is obtained, it is necessary only to slightly increase impulsion by yielding of the hand to arrive at passage.

At first, do not start from an elevated piaffer but from the small piaffer, well cadenced, so that the increase in impulsion will become, through yielding of the hand, forward movement instead of gaining height. This increase in impulsion, accompanied by a yielding of the hand will at first cause a loss of balance, which will be expressed by a few strides of cadenced trot followed by ordinary trot. Now let the horse trot freely for a few metres during the first lessons, then, halt and stroke him.

Later, when forward movement is obtained, seek 2nd degree collection in the first strides of cadenced trot, then halt whilst in it.

Now try to increase the number of strides at the cadenced trot, with halt in 2nd degree collection each time the cadence is lost. Next, go back to the piaffer and, once again, depart from the cadenced trot. Little by little, the horse will maintain the cadenced trot in 2nd degree collection during a greater number of strides. When the horse has found his equilibrium in this work, the start can be made from a higher piaffer, while making sure to maintain cadence in the forward movement.

Then, by increasing the impulsion which is received and held accurately and precisely by the hands, the elevation of the legs will be progressively increased with a longer time of suspension. Thus, the horse will go from the cadenced trot (or small passage) to the true passage, which will be more or less brilliant according to the horse's aptitudes, energy, suppleness and the skill of the rider. Above all, seek regularity, calm in the energy manifested and a cadence which is as slow as possible. It is preferable to retain the small passage longer, rather than trying to raise the action too rapidly to the detriment of the regularity of the gait, for it is always difficult to make bad habits disappear.

PASSAGE, STARTING FROM THE TROT

The passage can also be obtained by starting directly from the cadenced trot, without first going through the piaffer.

Cadencing the trot consists of obtaining a slower cadence than in the medium trot by seeking to prolong the legnth of time the diagonal is on the ground. As stated above, it is by weighting this diagonal that the length of time it is on the ground will be increased and, by this same fact, the time of elevation of the legs on the other diagonal. In this way, the rider will obtain a cadenced trot or small passage resembling the one already obtained by starting from the piaffer. Then, follow the steps indicated in the preceding section.

However, with regard to the foreleg which is on the ground, the bearing rein is not sufficient. At the same time, use a direct rein of opposition on the opposite side, for it is necessary to slow the horse at the same time. Therefore, for the right foreleg on the ground, use the right direct rein of opposition and the left bearing rein.

PIAFFER, STARTING FROM THE PASSAGE

Since the piaffer is nothing other than the passage in place, a piaffer can also be obtained starting from the passage. To do this, progressively slow the passage by alternating the normal passage with the slowed passage, while taking care to avoid abrupt transitions. Little by little, a few strides without moving forward will be obtained. Stop as soon as this happens and rest the horse in place.

While continuing the same work, now try to increase the number of strides of piaffer. Then, demand the piaffer starting from the halt when the horse has found his balance.

PIROUETTES AT THE CANTER

In the preceding period, the horse was prepared for pirouettes at the canter. Thus, it is now a question of demanding the pirouette starting directly from the canter.

In order to begin the pirouette under good conditions, it is necessary to precede it by a few strides of highly collected canter and, if possible, by one stride of canter in place. At first, do not try to execute complete pirouettes, but first start with quarter pirouettes followed by canter on the straight line. Then, progressively go to half-pirouettes, and finally to pirouettes.

In this work, the aids must be very precise and they should be used in the following manner (pirouette left to right, canter on the right leg):

1. While the left leg forms a wall to prevent the haunches from falling out to the left, the right leg maintains the impulsion.

2. The right hand acts as for the canter on the straight line, but with a slight opening rein action, and the left hand produces a rein of indirect opposition 4th effect at the time it would normally act. In summary, the right hand expresses the wish to displace the forehand toward the right and the left hand prolongs this wish by reinforcing it and obliging the horse to carry out the action.

The horse will respond all the better to the rider's demands as lightness is greater. It is very important to watch the mobility of the hindlegs, when the necessity of a great deal of impulsion. In order to facilitate this mobility of the hindlegs, it is indispensable, at first, to allow them to move on a small circle. The diameter of the circle will be progressively reduced.

A good pirouette fulfills the following criteria:

1. The three beats of the canter are well marked, and the cadence of the canter remains the same or diminishes only slightly.

2. The diameter of the circle described by the hindlegs is as small as possible and, in any case, less than 50 centimetres; for perfection consists of mobility in place of the hindlegs, but this perfection is difficult to obtain and must come very progressively. Above all, the horse must remain at the canter.

As in the pirouettes at the walk (turns on the haunches), there must be the feeling that the horse is bending around the rider's inside leg (right leg in the pirouette from left to right). In this way, the rider obtains a slight curving favourable to a good performance of the movement.

Pirouettes at the canter can be done in any direction, but it is a good idea to work on pirouettes in the following exercises:

1. With the horse at the canter in head-to-the-wall, demand a pirouette and then go on in head-to-the-wall.

2. During a turn across the width of the riding school at the canter on two tracks, demand a pirouette in the middle and then go on at the canter on two tracks. Upon arrival at the opposite side, go into a walk.

3. During a turn down the centre line down the length of the riding hall, do a pirouette at the centre point or at any point (do not forget to work on both hands).

4. During a turn across the width of the riding school do a pirouette on the quarter line, change leads at the centre point, do another pirouette in the opposite direction on the other quarter line.

SPANISH WALK AND TROT

These particularly brilliant Haute Ecole movements are not demanded at the Olympic Games. Actually, the basis of this training is almost always dismounted work and, for this reason, it only offers a very relative interest from the point of view of dressage properly speaking, since it is possible to use trickery.

I am only mentioning this here in order to touch on the subject, especially since riders who might be interested in this work will easily find all the information they wish in numerous works on equitation. However, I advise them not to grapple with these movements until their horse has received a rational training and is perfectly submissive and light. The epitome of dressage does not consist in executing seemingly brilliant movements with a contracted horse, lacking in lightness and obeying only forceful effects. Such work may sometimes impress uninformed spectators, but it presents no interest for those who know how to appreciate the beauty, harmony and grace which are the appanage of a light, supple horse, responding to the discreet actions of his rider.

PART IX

DEFENCES AND DIFFICULTIES

DEFENCES AND DIFFICULTIES

In spite of the rider's skill and a rational and correctly applied progression of training, do not believe that the training of the horse will be carried out without occasionally encountering difficulties, which are sometimes serious, or even defences.

In fact, although the horse has a character and temperament which make it possible to dominate him quite easily, he is, nevertheless, subject to more or less violent reactions which sometimes set the rider up against difficulties which may originate from various causes: character, conformation, physical suffering, or even bad habits inculcated by a clumsy trainer.

Therefore, it is indispensable to know the means the rider has at his disposal to fight the principal defences he may encounter.

In order to fight these defences, as a general rule, it is necessary to act differently if the horse is new, that is, beginning training, or if the horse has already worked and acquired bad habits. In the first case, try to be gentle and firm; in the second case, on the contrary, it is almost always necessary to use force to show the horse that he is no longer the master when he encounters a good rider.

STUBBORN RESISTANCE

Natural stubborn resistance is very rare when the first lessons on the lunge have been given correctly. However, if, at the very beginning, the rider feels that the horse has a tendency to stubbornness, it is indispensable to insist upon the lesson of the legs given on the lunge and to frequently return to it, if necessary. The important point is to be sure to reward with pats, oats, carrots and so on as soon as the horse shows good will. On the other hand, be sure to punish the horse as soon as there is rebellion, either with the lunge whip when he is on the lunge rein, or with the riding whip in other cases. Later, the correction can be given with the spurs when the horse is confirmed to their use.

Most of the time, stubborn resistance comes from either unwillingness or a faulty conformation. Any signs of stubborn resistance must be fought immediately by forward movement by the means already described. The movement which has provoked the resistance should not be taken up again until the rider feels that his horse is again completely submissive and, if necessary, the rider should be a little less demanding.

After the horse has been trained to the shoulder-in, do not forget to use this means of domination each time there is stubborn resistance.

Note the use of rigid reins recommended by the General l'Hotte. I have ascertained their efficiency on several horses.

REARING

This defence is quite often found in young horses which lack natural impulsion. It can become dangerous for the rider when the horse, getting too near the vertical, loses his balance and falls over backwards. The rider receives the mass of the horse upon him.

Nearly always, it is the rider who is the cause of the loss of equilibrium. If he does not have a solid seat, the upper part of his body is projected backwards and, in order to stay in the saddle, he hangs onto the reins, thus causing enough pulling from front to rear to bring about a loss of balance.

Given this fact, in such a situation, the rider's reflexes should make it possible for him to conform to the two principles stated below:

1. Lean forward as much as possible, while assuring a fixed position of the legs to bring about a preponderance of weight toward the front.

2. Bring the hands forward in order to leave the reins 'floating' and, thus, avoid any pulling on the horse's mouth.

It is evident that rearing must be fought as soon as it appears. And it is, again, by forward movement that it can be fought efficiently, for, if the horse flies forward upon the action of both legs, he cannot mark time at the halt, which necessarily precedes rearing. The leg action must be energetic and applied before rearing commences.

If the horse does not respond to the action of both legs and starts to rear, this can be fought by a wide opening rein, while avoiding any pulling to the rear and any action with the other rein. If this action is carried out rapidly, it will be enough to cause a loss of balance toward the side, which will force the horse to stop his rearing.

Another defence encountered in some horses is rearing and doing a half-turn, either to avoid forward movement or because of fear of an object. It should be noted that in this defence the half-turn is always to the same side, the rider should hold his whip on this side. When the half-turn takes place, he should suddenly raise the whip horizontally by rotating his wrist. Frightened by the sight of the whip, the horse will almost always stop his half-turn and put his forelegs back on the ground again. Then attack energetically with both legs.

When a horse rears before the rider has time to act, he should take the position described in 1 and 2 above and wait until the horse starts to bring his forehand down; this is the favourable moment to attack energetically with both legs without waiting until the forelegs have time to regain contact with the ground. Try to obtain the forward movement before the horse has time to rear again. If the leg action is not enough, use the whip at the same time to reinforce the action of the legs.

However, with an insufficiently confirmed young horse, the trainer may need to return to the lunge to teach the leg aids. If necessary, provoke the horse into rearing, so that the assistant may use the lunge whip energetically.

Some riders recommend empirical and brutal methods

which I have never seen used and which I do not advise. Nothing replaces rational training and rearing will disappear when complete submission to the action of both legs is obtained.

KICKING OUT

This defence is not dangerous. It is fought by energetic upward action of the hands to pick up the head and neck and to oppose the raising of the croup. In addition, avoid allowing the horse to become immobile. Depend on the forward movement in this case also.

Bucking is fought in the same way.

FRIGHTENED, TIMID HORSES

The rider should be patient with timid horses and never treat them roughly which would only aggravate the difficulty.

Since fear is not a question of unwillingness, above all, use all means to gain the horse's confidence. Out-of-doors, put him in the company of a calm horse and try to familiarise him with all the objects which provoke his fear. If necessary, dismount and lead him to the objects which frighten him, while patting him. Some of these objects can be put in his stable when this is possible.

However, when the training is well advanced and the horse is trained to the combined effect, do not neglect to use this. The combined effect, being a very powerful means of domination, makes it possible to put the horse at the complete disposal of his rider and gives surprising results with a frightened horse. It may be said that it is the most efficient means of dominating fear.

STARGAZERS

These horses fall into two categories:

1. The horse which stargazes because of faulty conformation (ewe-necked).

2. The horse which takes this position to evade the action of the rider's hand.

In the first case, it will be difficult to completely correct this fault, but it will be possible to improve it considerably. Training in flexions will make it possible to progressively modify the position of the head and the neck. In addition, work on the longe with Chambon reins gives excellent results by forcing the neck muscles to work in a lower position, in this way progressively bringing about an improvement in conformation.

In the second case, it is up to the rider to improve his hands, for, if the horse tries to avoid the action of the hands, this is because it is too hard and brutal. Therefore, it will be necessary to work on flexion training with hands which are more gentle and softer. It is also possible that the bit is too harsh and that it is necessary to replace it with a milder one.

In all of this work, it is indispensable to maintain the forward movement, if necessary with energetic legs.

HORSE BEHIND THE BIT

Horses behind the bit are those which refuse contact with the hand, arch their necks and bring their faces behind the vertical line to evade action of the bit.

The remedy to this fault consists in sending the horse forward with energetic leg action to force him to lengthen his neck. At first, be satisfied with a light contact on the bit with a very soft hand. Also be sure that the bit is not too harsh. In addition, demand 1st degree collection only with a raised neck.

HEAD-TOSSING

These horses are also trying to avoid the action of the hand, either because it is too harsh, or because the bit is not suitable to the horse's mouth. A young horse rarely tosses his head, if he has been properly started.

In order to correct this fault, the horse must hurt himself each time he tosses his head. To obtain this result, place the hand low, keep it steady and each time the horse wants to toss his head, quickly tighten the fingers on a fixed hand, so that the horse hits a fixed point. The resulting pain, by his own fault, will be a salutary lesson, which will make him hesitate before beginning again. Immediately afterwards, loosen the fingers and push with the legs.

JOGGING

Horses which jog may be classified in two different categories:

1. Those which do it through nervousness.

2. Those which walk with too short steps and cannot follow a horse with a normal walk.

In the first case, try to calm the horse with the voice and stroking and, if that is not enough, demand a few strides of shoulder-in to the right and to the left until the horse decides to walk. The rider must have a great deal of patience and calm; nervousness of the rider can only increase that of the horse.

In the second case, work the horse alone or with a horse which has the same walk.

Try to make him lengthen his walk by pushing with the legs and the seat and take advantage of the return to the stable to demand the maximum extension of the walk he can give. Progress will be slow and much patience and tenacity will be necessary.

RUNAWAY HORSES

In this category, one must consider the natural runaway horse, that is, the horse which takes advantage of any occasion to try to run away and, on the other hand, the horse which only runs away exceptionally because of clumsiness or an exaggerated demand on the part of the rider.

The horses in the second case are easy to cure, but, above all, avoid letting the horse become aware of his strength in such a case and immediately try to find means of dominating him.

How may a runaway horse be characterised? It is a horse which takes a hold on the bit and refuses obedience to any actions which the rider may try to produce with the bit, thus increasing the speed, which in a very short time becomes a very rapid rate that is impossible to moderate.

First of all, it is necessary to avoid provoking this defence by knowing how to measure the demands and preventing it by lateral and direct flexions.

It should be noted that a horse can run away at the trot, as well as at the gallop. Some riders even say that they have been run away with at the walk. Personally, I do not believe this, for, at this gait, the rider has powerful means of dominating his horse. On the other hand, at the trot and especially the gallop, the rider no longer has as much action upon the horse's mass.

With the horse which is not a true runaway, it is usually sufficient when this defence happens to raise the head and neck by an energetic half-halt, maintaining the hands high until the horse has yielded. I have tried this on a runaway horse and the defence disappeared in a few days.

However, this procedure will probably not be sufficient with a horse which has become a true runaway and the horse will respond by taking a stronger hold on the hand.

The particular conditions of the moment have a primary importance and oblige the rider to choose and decide upon the means to be used. Here is how I have proceeded under different circumstances.

One day, I was on a forest road with a horse of a very difficult character. He responded to my demands by taking hold of the bit. Then, refusing to yield in any way, he was soon going at a very fast gallop. Since I had a great deal of space and could gallop for several kilometres, I began by completely ceasing the action of my hands and I played dead on the horse's back. After about 1500 metres of this frenzied race, there was a rather long, steep hill, but, by this time, my horse slowed down and wanted to return to the walk. That was when I used my spurs and whip to prevent him from doing so. At the top of the hill, my horse stopped upon a voice command. I brought him back to the place where the incident happened and I obtained obedience to the demand which had caused the defence. From that time on, he never again tried to run away. This lesson had been a salutary one for him and corrected him forever.

Obviously, the rider does not always have enough space in front of him, so I shall describe another case which happened several times under particularly difficult circumstances.

This happened in a little outdoor arena situated in the centre of a garrison courtyard. I was riding a nervous and impressionable horse which I had been given to train because of his exceptional jumping ability.

A training course of stadium jumps was set up in the arena and I began training the horse over jumps. I was quite cautious, because he was considered a runaway and had been taken out of race training for that reason.

All went well at the beginning, but then he took my hand, jumped the bank surrounding the arena and dashed into the garrison courtyard in the middle of the buildings. I immediately loosened my fingers and remained still; otherwise, there would have been a catastrophe. I waited for a slight relaxation and as soon as it happened, I took advantage of it to carry out a strong lateral action. From that time on, my horse was dominated and let himself be stopped.

He tried the same thing again several times on that day. Each time, I used the same means and, after a short while, he gave up the defence. Two months later, he took part in stadium jumping competition in Paris under excellent conditions and later had brilliant results in several international jumping shows.

I shall give another example: a five-year-old Anglo-Arab being prepared for stadium jumping. This horse was a natural runaway. I had given him to experienced riders several times for trail rides and, although I had warned them, each time he ran away. So I decided not to give him to others to be ridden.

He often tried this defence with me but, each time, I had the time to prevent him by the use of lateral flexions or the shoulder-in.

The following lessons may be learned from these different examples:

1. The rider must remain watchful with such horses, constantly change contact to avoid their taking hold, relax the mouth with lateral and direct flexions, often do a few strides of shoulder-in, and know when to cease demands to be able to relax the horse before the defence can occur.

2. If the horse does run away the rider must, above all, remain calm, cease all action of his hands and sense the moment of natural relaxation, which will enable him to act rapidly and efficiently.

However, if the rider is dealing with a particularly difficult horse, with which these means are practically useless, it is necessary to find a bit which enables him to remain master. Colbert reins with a double snaffle can give good results with certain subjects. In this case, attach the draw reins to one snaffle and ordinary reins on the other. The rider uses the ordinary reins when the horse does not manifest his defence and, as soon as he feels that the defence is going to take place, he uses the other snaffle which acts on the corners of the mouth by means of the Colbert reins and, thus, brings about relaxation of the jaw. If these reins are not enough, take a snaffle with a controlling noseband, which should normally be effective, because it cuts off the horse's breathing when he pulls; in addition, it spares the bars.

The rider should use all the means that he may have at his disposal in order to correct this fault, which makes the horse unusable and dangerous. He could also use long-reins, which are a powerful means of domination and which can also bring about the horse's submission.

TAIL SWISHING

Tail swishing is a natural reaction, which happens with all horses at the approach of the spurs, when training to the spurs has been insufficient.

For this reason, from the start of training, try to avoid tail swishing by proceeding very gradually and by following the steps described below to gain the animal's confidence.

At first, be satisfied with the pressure of the calves, leaving them in contact until any movement of the tail has disappeared. Little by little, the horse will no longer pay attention to this. Then, lower the action as far as pressure of the heel (with no spurs). Then, when this action no longer causes any tail swishing, blunt spurs may be worn and the use of roweled spurs will progressively be reached. However, with some horses and especially sensitive mares, it is preferable to use only blunt spurs or spurs with dull rowels.

If there is a movement during the course of training which causes tail swishing, it is preferable to put off the demand and to continue to improve the horse's acceptance of the spurs, in order to avoid this bad contraction of muscles of the croup becoming a reflex at each approach of the legs.

CONCLUSION

This does not claim to reveal any secrets which any one could use in the training of a horse. Everything it contains is known by all riding masters deserving of the name. However, that which is less well known, especially by those who are learning dressage, is the logical progression of all the movements and the suppling exercises which bring the horse to the Haute Ecole, if the rider so desires.

From this point of view, it is presented in a form which will make it possible for any rider (who wishes to approach the question of dressage in a somewhat deeper manner) to avoid feeling his way and hesitating, which is often discouraging to those who are not lucky enough to have a good teacher.

It is obvious that the rider must know enough to understand the result obtained. It is just as necessary for a rider to 'feel' his horse as it is for a musician to have a good ear. Every rider, who knows how to feel and think, should obtain excellent results, if he follows the stated programmes exactly and takes into account the principles given therein.

In particular, do not forget that without impulsion there is no possible dressage, for one rapidly arrives at a refractory horse. In addition, it is primordial to know how to give. All riders know how to take, but there are very few who know how to give and yet that is the secret of lightness. The trainer must constantly watch himself.

In order to have a truly light horse, one must have the feeling of reins that are almost floating, except when the hand resists. The light horse must sustain himself on a steady leg contact. He then gives the impression of waiting for the rider's orders.

This lightness is the result of the horse being on the bit, which must be perfected during the course of dressage, first on circles with haunches-out, then on circles with haunches-in and last on the straight line. First at the walk, then at the trot and the canter. Lightness becomes perfect when collection is obtained.

Although this programme concerns only dressage properly speaking, it would be a serious error to conclude that obstacle training cannot be carried out at the same time. In fact, it is possible and even recommended, to work a horse over jumps during the course of dressage. By the same token, do not feel that it is necessary to remain between the four walls of a riding school; on the contrary, one must take the horse outside and across country as often as possible. During the course of these rides, one must take advantage of a suitable spot to practice some of the movements performed in the riding school. This outside work makes it possible to obtain a calm horse under all circumstances and, at the same time, keep the horse gay.

It should be noted that this programme is adaptable to all saddle horses, whatever their final use may be. Each rider may stop at the time he feels his horse is sufficiently instructed and that it has acquired the qualities desired for the work it will be asked to do. It is evident that, for a horse being prepared for combined training it will be unnecessary to bring it as far as the *Haute Ecole*. It will be sufficient for the horse to be able to perform as correctly as possible the required dressage test.

To work, riders. Be calm and persevering and I hope that the results which you obtain will be, for you, the source of great satisfaction which only patient, persistent and thoughtful riders can know.